By Jane Fonda

Being a Teen

Prime Time

My Life So Far

Women Coming of Age (with Mignon McCarthy)

Jane Fonda's New Workout & Weight-Loss Program

Jane Fonda's Workout Book

Being a Teen

Being a Teen

Everything Teen Girls & Boys Should Know About
Relationships, Sex, Love, Health, Identity & More

Jane Fonda

Random House New York

As you read through (or dip into) the pages that follow, please remember that no book can replace the diagnostic expertise and medical advice of a trusted physician. It is extremely important to consult with your doctor before making medical decisions, particularly if you are or think you may be pregnant, if you are experiencing pain or other symptoms of illness, or if you have ever been diagnosed with a medical condition that requires ongoing care.

In putting this book together, I have included some references to resources (including online resources) that I hope may be of help to teenage readers and their families. As of press time, the URLs displayed in this book link or refer to existing websites on the Internet, but of course Web addresses do change over time. Unfortunately, I cannot guarantee that any given resource will be useful or appropriate to you, and neither I nor my publisher should be understood to endorse the content of any third-party website or recommend the services of any particular provider. These references are intended for your information and to encourage you to begin your own search for resources that work for you.

A Random House Trade Paperback Original

Copyright © 2014 by Jane Fonda

Illustrations copyright © 2014 by Julia Rothman

Published in the United States by Random House Trade Paperbacks, an imprint of Random House, a division of Random House LLC, a Penguin Random House Company, New York.

RANDOM HOUSE and the HOUSE colophon are registered trademarks of Random House LLC.

LIBRARY OF CONGRESS CATALOGING-IN-PUBLICATION DATA
Fonda, Jane
Being a teen : everything teen girls & boys should know about relationships, sex, love, health, identity & more / by Jane Fonda.
pages cm
Includes bibliographical references and index.
ISBN 978-0-8129-7861-2
eBook ISBN 978-0-8129-9604-3
1. Teenage pregnancy. 2. Teenagers—Sexual behavior. 3. Sex instruction for teenagers. 4. Teenagers—Health and hygiene. I. Title.
RG556.5.F66 2014   618.200835—dc23   2013016042

Printed in the United States of America on acid-free paper

www.atrandom.com

2 4 6 8 9 7 5 3

Book design by Diane Hobbing

Author's Preface

A Word About This Book

For about seventeen years I've been working with teens around issues of sexuality, self-esteem, and relationships. I have a passion for this work, partly because when I was a teen I was very confused about all of this and didn't know where to go for answers. I also know it can be hard for adults and teens to talk about some of these important subjects. I've seen the bad things that can happen to a person—physically and emotionally—when he or she is not properly informed.

In the 1990s, I founded the Georgia Campaign for Adolescent Pregnancy Prevention (now called the Georgia Campaign for Adolescent Power & Potential) and the Jane Fonda Center for Adolescent Reproductive Health at Emory University School of Medicine. This book grows out of that work, and all my net proceeds from this book will go to these organizations.

I kept meeting teens across a wide economic and social spectrum who didn't understand enough about how their bodies worked, or didn't know who to ask, or how they could prevent getting pregnant or getting someone else pregnant, or didn't know how to avoid getting HIV/AIDS and other sexually transmitted infections (STIs). We were asked, over and over again in the program, questions like "How do I know if I'm in a real relationship?" and "How can I say 'no' and still be popular?" and "When is it okay to have sex?" There is so much misinformation about these things floating around that I felt that the health of many teens I met—their future happiness, even—was on the line. I wanted to write an honest book for teens that would be a frank and straightforward resource for them, for both boys and girls, and an aid for parents, teens, teachers, librarians, and others, in talking about sex, health, identity, and relationships. This book, written for teens, provides access to information that we found in the Georgia programs that many teens need today.

In the Georgia project, we found that one big reason many teenagers don't know all that they need to know about sex, relationships, and bodies is that people tend to worry about the things that can go wrong when it comes to sexuality, especially when a person is young. This can make the focus seem to be on the negatives—the dangers of sex, and how to avoid them.

However, most experts on sexuality and adolescence—the teenage years—think it is a mistake to focus just on the negatives and not talk about communication, relationships, and how beautiful and exciting sexuality *can* be. There is no evidence that talking about the realities of sex encourages a person to have sexual intercourse. In fact, when you understand how precious and beautiful sexuality *can* be, you are less likely to engage in sexual acts you're not ready for or that make you uncomfortable. You are also more likely to make healthy decisions and use protection when you do choose to have sexual intercourse. The pleasurable aspect of sex is also discussed here, as a key to making healthy decisions about whether or when to have sex, and to knowing whether the people in one's life are respecting you, your wishes, and your needs.

Many schools offer classes about sexuality and the changing teen body. Some provide information about the body, birth control, and STIs. This book is about those things, and more—about feelings and fears, about the culture in which we live, and about what a real, loving relationship is.

Jane Fonda
September 2013

Foreword

by Melissa Kottke, M.D., M.P.H., M.B.A.

Every person has a unique path to understanding his or her body, sexuality, health, and relationships. Jane Fonda has been linking young people to essential information about these topics for decades. She has spent more than twenty years educating herself on health, sexuality, and relationships, and has worked with doctors, health professionals, educators, program directors, policymakers, religious and spiritual leaders, other advocates, and teens themselves on these important issues. Most people know of Jane Fonda as an Academy Award–winning actress, fitness guru, and advocate, but this book gives readers the opportunity to know her as a guide and teacher. In *Being a Teen,* Jane takes on one of her most important roles, and one that means a great deal to her: that of giving facts to young people to help them succeed.

Already a longtime advocate for young people's health, Jane Fonda founded the Georgia Campaign for Adolescent Pregnancy Prevention (GCAPP) in 1995. GCAPP has been the central organization championing teen pregnancy prevention in the state of Georgia, working through education, training, and special programming. A few years later, Jane started the Jane Fonda Center for Adolescent Reproductive Health at Emory University, to join academic partners in research to advance the field of adolescent sexual and reproductive health. In 2001, she dedicated a special teen-clinic space at Grady Memorial Hospital in Atlanta, Georgia, where best practices in clinical care and education are delivered to teens in need. Jane fosters the work of these organizations and institutions through direct involvement and cultivation. Through these three organizations, tens of thousands of teens have directly received clinical care and programming and at least a dozen curricula and educational tools have been developed. Hundreds of thousands of people have benefited from the education and training delivered by these organizations. Thanks to the work that Jane has spearheaded regarding teen pregnancy in Georgia, our state has witnessed declines in teen birth at a rate that is among the highest in the country!

I first met Jane Fonda in 2005, when I was interviewing for a job as Director of the Jane Fonda Center. I had just finished a fellowship in family planning and contraception at Emory, and prior to that a residency in obstetrics and gynecology at the University of Texas Southwestern Medical Center. At first I was a bit intimidated to meet her, but that feeling faded quickly as Jane and I talked about what motivated us both—giving young people the information and tools they needed to navigate the transition to adulthood safely and healthily. Her level of engagement and her detailed knowledge about adolescent reproductive health immediately impressed me. We have been working together ever since.

In *Being a Teen,* Jane covers every topic young people need to know about, from puberty to bullying and beyond. She addresses a wide spectrum of subjects, from basic concepts to more advanced and abstract ideas, providing details about physical "stuff," like body parts, hormones, periods, hygiene, contraception, and STIs, as well as nonphysical "stuff," like dealing with parents, values, friendship, gender issues, the media, self-esteem, sexual orientation, abuse, and eating disorders. Additional resources for more information are provided throughout the book, frequently at the end of a chapter. This broad approach makes *Being a Teen* a useful guide for any teen that can be referenced again and again as new questions arise.

Jane knows that young people need reliable information and that facts are crucial to their health and happiness. In *Being a Teen,* as in her day-to-day life, she is fearless and straightforward. Jane is bold in her support of happiness, communication, and honesty. She writes for males and females, and shows how one needs to understand the other. She talks about pregnancy and STI prevention and sets high expectations for personal responsibility. She also presents the building blocks toward understanding one's self, and beginning down the path of incorporating one's sexuality in a healthy and positive manner. Jane offers the sage advice "If you have a good relationship with yourself, it's easier to have a good relationship with others." This is a truth that takes most of us years to learn.

Jane has a deep understanding of how important it is for young people to understand the changes they are experiencing, how to protect themselves, and how to love themselves. Jane operates with the belief that knowledge is power. Through *Being a Teen,* she continues this important work and expands her reach. This thorough, frank, and necessary book will be an indispensable tool for both young people and their parents.

Melissa Kottke, M.D., M.P.H., M.B.A.

Director, Jane Fonda Center at Emory University

Assistant Professor, Emory University
Department of Gynecology and Obstetrics

Medical Director, Teen Services Program
at Grady Memorial Hospital

Contents

II
Your Body

4 Boys' Sexual and Reproductive Parts and How They Function 35

5 Girls' Sexual and Reproductive Parts and How They Function 51

6   Changes in Both Girls and Boys That You Can See   67

III
Sexuality

12   Sexual Orientation and Gender Identity   136

15   Sexual Abuse

IV
Important Relationships

List of Illustrations

Being a Teen

1.

What This Book Is All About

Your Developing Identity

This is an important time in your life. Who you are as a person—your identity—is being developed, and you are beginning your lifelong journey of personal sexual understanding and expression. By identity, I mean your values, your beliefs, what you like and don't like, how you treat others, and how you treat yourself. Yet this is also a time when there are so many pressures to be how others want you to be. You may be tempted to be different from who you really are so that you'll be popular with a certain group, or seem cool.

Sexuality is not just about body parts, STIs, and contraception. It is also a large part of a person's identity, and that is why this book is also about relationships and feelings. How you understand and deal with them will help form your identity. I also write about the media and culture because they, too, can influence your identity—and not always for the good.

Adolescence is the gateway to adulthood, a stage of life filled with changes, with its own unique joys and challenges. In this book, I've tried to address the *whole* you, all the different parts—the physical, mental, and emotional things that are part of the adult person you are becoming.

Key Ideas I Hope You'll Learn

Here are the key ideas I hope you'll learn from this book:

1. This is the time in your life when you should begin to really know who you are as a person, who you want to be, what values you claim for yourself. Knowing who you are will help you make decisions that are right for *you.*
2. Your body is still developing and you have a right to understand how it is changing. Your body is not to be feared, nor should you feel shame or guilt about it, no matter what.
3. Abstaining from sexual intercourse when you are young is the best way to reduce your risk of pregnancy and infection—of course!
4. Do not start having sex just because your friends say they are sexually active.
5. You can say "no" to any form of sex—kissing, touching, anything—*anytime you feel like it, for any*

reason. Boys and girls are both responsible for seeking each other's permission before any sexual touching advances.

6. If you start having sex, be sure you are able to discuss contraception with your partner and use it correctly *every single time.*

7. Being with someone you trust and can communicate with, besides someone who turns you on, helps ensure your experience will be pleasurable. Young men and women are both responsible for talking about feelings and asking about feelings.

8. If you have been sexually abused, assaulted, or harassed, it was not your fault. You need to talk right away with a trusted adult and tell them what has happened to you.

This Is a "Dip-in" Book

You don't need to read this book from start to finish—although I hope you will. You may prefer to dip in and out of this book, or read the parts you most want to know about. Flipping to topics of particular interest to you is fine, and I've structured the book that way. I hope you enjoy it and learn from it.

I

Your Identity: Who You Are and How You Feel About Yourself

2.

Your Relationship with Yourself

There is no doubt the most important relationship we have is our relationship with ourselves. By that I mean having a sense of your own values; starting to have a sense of what your strengths and weaknesses are; feeling that your actions accurately reflect who you are and not just things you do because other people want you to or just to please others. There's nothing wrong with pleasing others, but not if that betrays who you are. If you have a good relationship with yourself, it's easier to have a good relationship with others. Later in this book we'll talk about relationships with family and friends.

Puberty

Your awareness of self as a separate individual usually begins during puberty. Puberty is the biological part of the early adolescent years, when the sexual and reproductive systems start to mature. For some, puberty starts even sooner and for others it can start later. Some of you in high school will still be going through puberty. Boys usually go through puberty one or two years later than girls do—between ages eleven and fifteen. Each person goes through puberty in different ways at different times, which is normal.

Your Teen Years

Your teen years begin at age thirteen and end around nineteen or twenty—when you have a completely adult body, though not yet a completely adult brain. The final development of your brain—the really important part in the front of your brain that handles decision making and planning—won't be complete for a few more years, around ages twenty-four or twenty-five.

Besides all the visible and invisible changes that are happening to your body, your personality is changing as well—how you think, how you feel, and how you relate to other people.

Thoughts and Feelings

At your stage of life, there is a lot of worrying about how you look, whether you come across as cool or nerdy, whether you are dressing right, whether your hairstyle is what it should be to make you look your best, whether your body is developing fast enough or too fast, whether you are popular, whether you should start hooking up.

Thinking in New Ways

During early puberty, a person's thoughts are likely to be mainly about what is happening right at the moment, not what might happen someday—what is known as "concrete thinking." In puberty, it's common to begin to think more about big things, such as your future. Arguing positions, exploring possibilities, considering new ideas and moral issues, is called "abstract thinking." Abstract thinking has a lot to do with your developing identity.

Thinking About Who You Are: Your Identity

Maybe you've begun to examine the values and beliefs that you've been brought up with. You are starting to think more for yourself and, as you continue to learn and grow over the years, you'll notice that things you feel sure of today may change many times.

During your teenage years is the time when your identity

is being developed—who you are as a person, on your own, separate from your parents and friends. Because you are just getting to know who you are, it's easy to be influenced by what others think of you—classmates, teachers, coaches. It's a good time to appreciate who you really are instead of what others want you to be. Think about the ways that you are different from your friends and family and the ways you are the same. Try writing them down, in a notebook just for you. Sometimes, when you write things down, it's easier to think about them, analyze them, and feel sure of opinions.

What kind of person are you, or do you want to be? Do any of these words come to mind: kind, considerate, generous, honest, loving, funny, smart? I didn't ask what you wanted to *do* in your life; rather, my question is about your *being*—how you'd like to *be* in the world. Write down the things you'd like to be and from time to time think about whether or not your actions, the friends you choose, and the things you do are contributing to your becoming this person.

Self-Esteem (Confidence)

Your adult identity is being created and you are developing self-esteem. *Self-esteem* means having positive feelings about yourself. This is different from what others think about you. Self-esteem comes from inside yourself. What are you good at? Sports? School? Music? Making people laugh? Putting things together? Cooking? Writing? Helping others? Drawing? Being a good friend? Think about trying to get better at the things

you're already good at. It helps our self-esteem when we know we have skills and qualities that are valuable no matter what anyone else says.

People who say mean things to other people have their own problems. They may not be nice people or they may just be having a bad time themselves. Maybe you've said mean things yourself.

Ask yourself if maybe the person who's being mean is jealous of you or has a reason to upset you. Maybe he or she doesn't feel very good about him- or herself and acts mean to feel more powerful. What we can do at times like these is think about our good qualities—think positively. Positive thoughts can become a habit and help develop self-esteem. What we mustn't do is base our feelings about ourselves on what other people say or do to us.

Young people who are passionate about things like music, drama, drawing, robotics, horseback riding, writing, and volunteering, and are involved in those activities, show more self-esteem. Girls and boys who engage in sports and fitness are less likely to have low self-esteem or engage in risky behaviors.

Everyone in the world has times of self-doubt, but this is a good time to learn ways to begin to overcome self-doubts and raise your self-esteem. For one thing, try to notice the people and situations that make you feel bad, and avoid them. Take different routes. On the other hand, think of the people and situations that make you feel good, and try to make them more a part of your life.

You may meet people who seem to have too much self-esteem. This probably means that underneath their cocky "I'm the best" attitude, they don't really have a lot of confidence.

Don't let anyone make you feel ashamed of who and what you are. Whatever your gender, race, beliefs, body shape, sexual orientation, economic status, or religion, no one can or should make you feel less than anyone else.

Moods

Your body is producing a lot of new hormones—*estrogen* in girls and *testosterone* in boys. These are what cause some of the mood swings that are so common in puberty and adolescence—perhaps more for girls than for boys.

If you feel sad and depressed for more than a week or so, try to talk to an adult who you know will listen to you. Hopefully you have the kind of relationship with one or both of your parents or a guardian that would make it easy to discuss your feelings with them. Maybe it's hard for them to start such a conversation. Maybe you're the one who has to get it going. If it's hard for you to talk to your parents, seek out another adult you trust who has proved wise and caring. Maybe there's a relative, a teacher, a coach, the parent of a friend, or a religious leader whom you like and who cares about you. Often just having someone listen to you can lift your spirits.

Drama

Chances are you are experiencing more drama or stress in your life now. It might make your body feel tense. You might feel nervous or anxious. Now is a good time to begin to notice when you feel stressed and cranky. See how drama makes you act and learn to manage it rather than acting out or just trying to live with it.

Ways to Cope

Exercise and Depression
Depression can take many forms in teenagers. You may feel sad or hopeless, have difficulty sleeping or concentrating, have low energy, have lost interest in things you like to do. You may feel grumpy or irritable. If there is a history of depression in

your family, you may be at higher risk for depression. Try to talk to an adult who you know will listen. Exercise and sports are a good way to make yourself feel better when you're down. Aerobic exercise—running, jogging, swimming, dancing, and biking—produces feel-good chemicals in your body called *endorphins*. You can actually feel the good sensation after 30 minutes or more of these activities.

Sleep

Often stress can be caused by lack of sleep. Sleep is really important at your age. You actually need *more* sleep now, to maintain alertness, than you did before puberty. Make it a priority. Experiment with ways that can help. For instance, drink a cup of warm milk right before bed. Milk contains a natural amino acid called *tryptophan* that is calming. Try not to eat or drink things in the evening that contain caffeine, such as chocolate and soft drinks. Starting about a half hour before you want to go to bed (and get those nine to ten hours), begin to relax, listen to soothing music, do things that you find calming. Deep breathing is an excellent way to make your body and mind relax and calm down. Roughhousing right before bedtime may be fun but it won't help you get ready to sleep. Turning off electronics thirty to sixty minutes before bed will help. Ask your parents to help you with all this.

Resource

www.teenmentalhealth.org

3.

Identity and the Culture You Live In

A lot of how we feel about ourselves is influenced by our culture, so it's important to become more aware of what the culture you live in is and how it may affect you.

What Is Culture?

Culture is a combination of the ideas, behaviors, and values of a society. We learn to interpret life through the lens of the culture we live in. You can't always see it, but culture is what tells us (and our parents and friends) how men and women, boys and girls, are supposed to be, look, and act.

The Media

The media—television, radio, film, music, newspapers, magazines, the Internet, advertising—is part of the culture, probably the part that you interact with the most, the part that has the potential to influence you the most.

Many of your thoughts and ideas come from outside you—from the media. Some of what you see and hear in the media is wonderful, but some of it is not so good, especially in terms of the messages it sends about gender roles—how women and men are supposed to be.

Much of the media is created by people and corporations whose main goal is to make money, and the ideas they put across may or may not be the right ideas for you. You don't want them to "have" you, to have power over you, do you? Probably not, so this is a good time to think about who you are, who you want to be, and what the media is telling you to be.

Mainstream Culture

The general culture we live in is referred to as "mainstream" culture. It is not set in stone. Every decade or so culture tends to change—sometimes a little, sometimes a lot. For example, when I was growing up in the forties, fifties, and early sixties, we saw only white people in TV commercials and on popular TV shows. We never heard women speaking in TV commercials, even those that promoted products used by women. News broadcasters were all white men. White men and male voices were considered more authoritative and were the only voices we heard. On the radio, in movies, and on television, women characters almost never worked outside the home. They did "women's work," which meant they were housewives—period! In the fifties and sixties, male models in magazines or TV ads were not all buffed up with six-pack abs and female models were not nearly as skinny as they are today. These are just a few examples of cultural change.

One huge change is how much more media teens are consuming today than ever before because of the new technologies—more TV channels, iPhones, iPads, and so forth. Because of this, the media is likely to have more influence over you than ever before.

Your Gender Identity

This is the time in your life when you begin to develop a gender identity. Sex is different from gender identity. Sex refers to biology—whether you have a penis or a vagina. Gender identity, on the other hand, is about how you feel about being male or female, how you feel you should behave as a male or female. Some people are asexual, meaning that they feel healthiest by not behaving as any one sex or engaging in anything sexual.

As I write about in Chapter 12, some people do not fit into these two distinct gender categories. They may be *transsexual, transgender, androgynous* (having characteristics of both masculinity and femininity at the same time), or still questioning their gender identity. Unfortunately, our mainstream culture will make that especially challenging for them by excluding them or unfairly portraying those who don't fit into "boy" or "girl" categories.

Regardless of how you identify, we are all very much alike. Whether you're a girl, boy, trans, questioning, or androgynous, you probably want to be liked, to have friends. We all fear not being experienced enough, being judged, and sometimes suffer "performance anxieties" (not being able to live up to expectations). However, the media often focuses on the differences between girls and boys. There are some important differences—besides the obvious biological ones. Let me try to explain.

Culture and Girls

When they are younger, most girls (if they're lucky) don't think too much about how they look, or about being popular and fitting in. They're just themselves.

What happens to many girls at puberty, when their bodies are developing and they become more aware of what girls are supposed to be like, is often described as "the loss of her true, authentic self." This does not happen to all girls, and it doesn't always happen at the same age. But it happens to many girls and they may not even be aware of it. The media plays a big role in this.

Losing Your True Self

Can you think of some way that the culture tries to make you hide or betray who you really are, in order to be what the culture suggests you should be?

Starting now, don't waste time being anything other than your authentic, true self. Can you think of ways you might do this? I want to say it again: This loss of true self does not happen to all girls. And it doesn't always happen at the same age. But it happens to many girls and it's important to be aware of it.

Cultural Messages to Girls

Our culture can make a girl start feeling pressure to

- be sexy
- fit in
- silence herself
- be a pleaser
- wear the "right" clothes or brands
- look "good" and conventionally beautiful
- have the right hair
- be passive rather than active
- be nice rather than honest
- do whatever it takes to be popular
- be a "lady"
- be unselfish
- not show it if she is angry
- not let on how smart she is
- have (and keep) a boyfriend
- be thin

What others can you think of? What pressures do you feel?

Here's another real-life example of how this can look: A psychologist named Catherine Steiner-Adair was doing research on girls in a middle school and sometimes she'd invite her students out for pizza. When she would ask the girls what they wanted on their pizzas, the ten-year-olds would want double cheese with pepperoni, the thirteen-year-olds would say, "I don't know," and the fifteen-year-olds would answer, "whatever you want." (Catherine Steiner-Adair and Lisa Sjostrom, *Full of Ourselves: A Wellness Program to Advance Girl Power, Health, and Leadership,* New York: Teachers College Press, 2005, p. 61.)

Girls can lose confidence when they hide what they really want and who they really are.

How Do You Want to Be Loved?

During adolescence, I thought that only a small portion of myself would be lovable, that if I wasn't perfect no one would love me. This made me very unhappy. I developed an eating disorder and suffered from depression. Later I learned to ask myself: "Do you want to be loved or do you want an image of yourself to be loved?" How you answer this question can have an impact on the rest of your life.

All of us want to be popular, to have friends. But you are at a time in your development when you need to decide: Is it worth abandoning your true self in order to be super popular or is it better to be true to who you are even if it means you may not be the most popular girl in your class? Notice if the values at this stage of your life seem to be way too much about the outside instead of the inside, where it really counts.

Culture and Boys

If many girls lose their true "voice" at puberty, for boys, it can be when they are very young. At five or six years old, at the start of their formal schooling, boys may have begun to receive messages from the mainstream culture that caused them to lose touch with their feelings.

Cultural Messages to Boys

It may have been from parents, teachers, a coach, or the media that boys got messages about what it takes to be a "real" man:

- Don't be a sissy.
- Real men don't cry.
- Don't be a momma's boy.
- Don't show your feelings.
- Don't ask for help.
- Be tough no matter what.

These are the messages that can make you start to act in the way that you think a man is supposed to be, maybe not who you really are.

A mainstream cultural message to boys is that it's manly to bully people who are different—perhaps people who are smaller, unathletic, unconventional looking, nerdy, vulnerable, or poor. The boys who engage in bullying are often the ones who are uncertain about their own manhood and cover it by violence and bullying. Or they feel that they have to bully to be popular.

If a man thinks he has to shut down his heart, cut himself off from feelings in order to prove he is a man, it will make it harder for him to have intimate relationships. Close, emotional relationships are healthy and fun. They make it easier to be happy, survive hardships, and enjoy life.

Make a list of all the messages you have received about what it means to be a man. (Some examples are to be brave, macho, tough, a leader, in control, to never walk away from a fight, not to cry, not to let others see your needs, to be a team player, and more.) Some messages are good ones and some aren't. Write them down. Then, when you've done that, go down the list and think about where you got each message. Was it from what you see and hear from the media? Was it from your father or a coach or a teacher or other guys? It's a good thing to realize that many of the ideas bubbling around in your brain come from outside yourself, and they may or may not be right for you. Maybe they are but maybe they aren't, and it's good to know the difference. It's important to learn to look inside yourself and see the good person you are and then to see the difference between those good qualities and some of the not-so-good qualities on your list.

Getting in Touch with Your Feelings
Dr. Michael Kimmel writes many books for boys and men. Here is what he tells his son Zach when they talk about how a boy needs to manage all the cultural messages he is receiving about being a man: "I tell him to imagine a boat on stormy seas, buffeted back and forth by forces that are stronger than he is. You have to steer clear of danger, but you can't just drift with the tide. You have to be active, steer the boat, take it where you want it to go, to that safe harbor."

One way to steer your boat is to think about emotions—

your own and other people's. When you do this it makes you more capable of *empathy*.[1] Here are three things that can help you do this:

- Try naming your feelings, such as sad, nervous, excited, or happy. Also melancholy and wistful—two examples of in-between emotions—not just happy or sad.
- Identify what other people are feeling by their facial expression, the tone of their voice, their body language.
- Try to identify what events or situations create certain emotions. For example, do you find that when you've lost someone or something important to you, you feel sad, or that it causes you to become angry or feel threatened?

Learning about your emotions will help you now, and also when you are older. It can help repair hurt feelings, solve relationship problems at home or at work, and maintain strong bonds with friends, spouses, and children over your lifespan.

Boys Compared with Girls

Another thing that our mainstream culture does is encourage the idea that boys are somehow superior to girls. This is apparent when a man feels it's okay to hit a woman, to view her as a weaker or inferior person, or to have sex with a woman even when she has said "no." It can cause boys to think girls should be available, passive, not too smart, always sweet, not strong

---

[1] Empathy is feeling others' feelings, putting yourself in others' shoes.

and assertive. Often, when a woman speaks her mind she is called a bitch. When a man does, he is called forceful.

Looking down on, disrespecting, females is a large part of our popular culture. It is all around us and it is harmful not just to females but ultimately to boys and men as well. If you grow up assuming this attitude is okay, you may have a hard time having a happy, loving relationship with a woman and with children and you will be numbing the human, tender, loving parts of yourself.

Boys are not better than girls just as girls are not better than boys. You are both wonderfully different. Yet, at the same time, each human being has a little of the male and a little of the female. This is normal and healthy.

Now is the time in your development when you need to become aware of aspects of mainstream culture that are disrespectful and dehumanizing and not let them influence you. This may not be easy. Boys who remain sensitive, emotional, and kind to girls may be teased and called names and may lose some of their female friends, too. You may be afraid that if you tell your friends to stop behaving disrespectfully toward girls they'll stop being your friends. And maybe they will. But you are entering a time in your life when you are beginning to define your identity, your values as a person, as a man. Think about whether you want to hang with boys who don't treat girls, or other people in general, with respect.

How to Move Forward
More and more men—athletes, doctors, teachers, actors, politicians, firefighters, all kinds of men—are fighting against the culture's toxic view of masculinity. They speak out in many

ways—through organizations, books, documentaries, public policies, and in the way they raise their sons—about what's wrong with the old myths about manhood. At the end of this chapter I give a list of some of these organizations and books. They point out that "real men" are those who are brave enough to respect and speak up on behalf of their female friends and other males who may be "different."

Just as real girls can be strong, smart, and able to change tires and fix things, boys can be strong, smart, and sensitive. They can prefer to read a book or write a song or a poem than play football. They can be a girl's best friend and not think they have to pressure her into having sex. They can walk away from a bully instead of feeling obliged to fight back. They can do all these things and still be masculine. A boy can be strong *and* sensitive, brave *and* vulnerable.

The Media and Sex

A lot of what is shown in the media relates to sex, and it is often an exaggerated, unrealistic view of it. Think about what this does to your own attitudes about sex. Do you feel that you should look and act sexy all the time to attract someone's attention? Do you believe that you need to be sexier or to have sex to be popular and fit in? Do you think sex is the most important part of life? Has the media caused you to think about sex in a casual way so that you don't worry about the consequences because you can just laugh it off?

In reality, sex can be a beautiful experience, but the media distorts it, blows it out of proportion, in order to manipulate you into watching a particular movie or TV show, buying something that you think will make you sexier and more popular, trying to be like somebody you see in magazines, on TV, or in the movies.

It's in your best interest to avoid being tricked by the media. Take a step back when you read or watch these sorts of messages in advertising, movies, television shows, and You-Tube videos, and when you hear the lyrics in many popular songs and see what's posted on social media sites. These are distorted messages that do not really represent the way teenagers and young adults interact with each other. For most of you, relationships and sex are not nearly as casual as these messages would make you think. Remember that they're playing with your mind and start resisting the influence.

Double Standard

What can be very confusing, especially for girls, is that we live in a sexualized culture, yet there is a double standard. The media encourages girls to look and act sexy, but society, in general, expects them to remain "virtuous," "virginal" "good girls." Look sexy but don't act sexy. It isn't easy to know who you really are as a sexual person in the midst of these conflicting messages.

As I write about in Chapter 11, this can cause a girl to ignore or hide her sexual desires; to disconnect from her own body and its feelings. This is called "disassociation." Disassociation can be dangerous because when a girl doesn't feel her own desire within her body, she may do sexual things just to please someone else. Girls who are very clear about what they feel and want are more able to say "no" and mean it. If you can't say "no" and mean it, you can't say "yes" and mean it, either.

Pornography

Pornography (sometimes called "porn") is also part of the media. Its job is to make money, and it makes billions of dollars a year. There are many concerns with pornography, especially if it is your main source of sex education. You risk learning from porn how to be in a sexual relationship, what is sexy, how to look and act. Boys may end up only wanting partners who look like porn stars. Girls may think they need to agree to have sex with another female in order to please a man.

The sex portrayed in most pornographic films is without caring, trust, or intimacy between the partners, the very things that can make sex wonderful. Further, it focuses only on the physical parts of sex and ignores the emotional and mental parts.

If, by some chance, you do watch porn, try to remember that it is not real, not a documentary. There is a script and editing. Don't confuse the impersonal, staged behaviors you see there with how sexuality ought to be in real life: loving, intimate, and mutually satisfying.

Step back from mainstream media and see which are the good parts and which are not. Doing this is sort of like getting vaccinated against the negative parts of the culture.

Resources

For Girls

- Rookie: An online magazine for girls and teens that covers a wide range of topics from music, movies, technology, love, sex, and more from a progressive, feminist perspective. http://rookiemag.com/

- V-Girls: "A global network of girl activists and advocates empowering themselves and one another to change the world, one girl at a time. Inspired by Eve Ensler's bestselling book *I Am an Emotional Creature: The Secret Life of Girls Around the World,* V-Girls is a platform for girls to amplify their voices and ignite their activism." http://www.v-girls.org/

- The Dressing Room Project: "A girl-powered rebellion to free girls and women from the bonds of media-imposed standards of beauty!" http://www.thedressingroomproject.org/index.html

- The Spark Movement: "A girl-fueled activist movement to demand an end to the sexualization of women and girls in media." They collaborate with hundreds of girls ages thirteen to twenty-two and more than sixty national organizations. www.sparksummit.com

- *New Moon Girls:* A magazine written by and for girls ages eight to fourteen, with intelligent and fun articles about issues important to girls. www.newmoon.com/magazine

For Boys

- Boys to Men International: Initiation weekends and follow-up mentoring for boys ages twelve to seventeen. www.boystomen.org

- Boys to Men New England: www.boystomennewengland.org

- *The Dangerous Book for Boys* by Conn Iggulden and Hal Iggulden, William Morrow, 2012.

- *100 Things Guys Need to Know* by Bill Zimmerman, Free Spirit Publishing, 2011.

- *Boys' Stuff: Boys Talking About What Matters* by Wayne Martino and Maria Pallotta-Chiarolli, Allen & Unwin, 2001.

II

Your Body

4.

Boys' Sexual and Reproductive Parts and How They Function

I've met lots of high school boys who didn't have enough accurate information about their own body and its reproductive parts, which is why I'm including this information.

I believe it is important to know and use the correct names for your body parts. Calling things by their proper names helps you to honor and "own" them. It's easier to give away that which you do not respect. This may also motivate you to protect and care for your own sexuality.

But perhaps you do know all you need to know about these things. If that's the case, you can skip these next chapters and go on to Chapter 6.

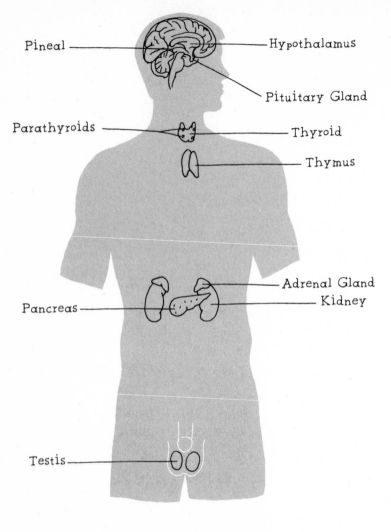

Male Endocrine System

Hormones

Puberty[1] is caused by hormones. Hormones are made by different *glands* in your body that are part of the body's *endocrine system*.[2] A gland is a group of cells that produce chemicals and hormones. Hormones act as messengers that travel through the bloodstream from these glands. Different hormones go to different glands and tell them what to do. By raising and lowering the levels of various hormones at different times, the endocrine system controls the body's functions and makes sure that they run together smoothly.

The body has many kinds of hormones. The two most important sex hormones, *testosterone* and *estrogen,* are produced by both males and females, but, starting at puberty, girls make much more estrogen and boys make much more testosterone. Testosterone is made in a male's *testicles,*[3] or balls.

Male Genitals

With puberty, and because of all the new hormones that are being produced, the *penis,*[4] testicles, and *scrotum*[5] begin to grow.

---

[1] puberty (**pyoo**-ber-tee): the biological part of the early adolescent years when the sexual and reproductive systems start to mature

[2] endocrine (**en**-duh-krin) system

[3] testicles (**tes**-ti-kuhls) or Testes (**tes**-teez): testicles are made up of a number of compartments, more commonly known as "balls," inside of which are tiny tubes, all intertwined.

[4] penis (**pee**-nis): the male reproductive organ

[5] scrotum (**skroh**-tuhm): the soft pouch of wrinkly skin that you see on either side and slightly behind your penis that is divided inside into two pouches. Each

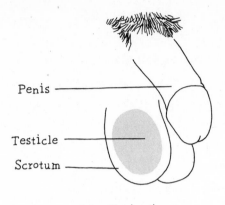

Penis ——————

Testicle ——————

Scrotum ——————

Male Genitalia

The scrotal sac hangs lower and becomes more wrinkled. Its color begins to change: darker with boys who have dark complexions and reddish for fair-skinned boys.

The Penis

Hanging down over the scrotum is the penis, a spongy tissue filled with blood vessels and nerves inside a soft tube of skin. (There is no bone inside the penis!) The penis has two parts. The *shaft* is the longer part; at the end of the shaft is the *glans* or *head*. At the tip of the glans or head is the *urethral opening*,[6] through which urine passes out of the body.

At other times, in ejaculation, a white, sticky fluid called *semen*[7] carries *sperm* (the male reproductive cell) out of the

---

pouch holds one testis. Many people refer to the scrotum and testes altogether as the testicles, or "balls."

[6] urethral (yoo-**ree**-thruhl) opening

[7] semen (**see**-muhn): the whitish fluid full of nutrients and sugar that comes out of the penis during an erection and contains 300 to 500 million sperm cells that contain chromosomes. Any sperm cell can make a female pregnant if intercourse occurs. Semen is sometimes called "cum" or "jism" or "jiz" in slang.

urethra as well. Urine and semen never come out the urethra at the same time. The connection to the bladder closes off just as the semen comes out of the penis.

Penises look different from one another in all kinds of ways:

- They can be different lengths, widths, and shapes. When erect, the penis may curve up, down, left, or right. All of this is normal.
- The tip of the penis can hang above or below the scrotum, or to the left or right of it.
- Some penises have veins showing on them, and others don't.

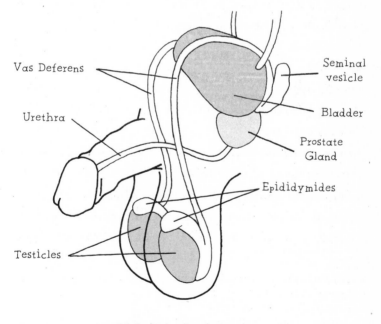

Male Reproductive Parts

- The skin can have papules,[8] small, shiny pink bumps around the head of the penis, (the *glans*). Younger men, and men with darker skin, are more likely to have papules, which may disappear over the years.

Foreskin

All males are born with a *foreskin*,[9] a loose sheath of skin that covers the glans. The foreskins of some boys are removed right after birth in a procedure called *circumcision*.[10] When the penis is erect, the foreskin pulls back, exposing the glans. If you are not circumcised, be sure you get into the habit of regularly pulling the foreskin back and cleaning underneath it.

The male foreskin produces a natural lubricant called *smegma*[11] that helps it slide smoothly. If you let smegma build up under your foreskin, it can start to smell bad. The glans and foreskin lining are very sensitive and soap might irritate them. Just rinse off the smegma.

Circumcision

In Muslim, Jewish, and other cultures, boys' foreskins are removed in the practice called circumcision. In some cultures (not in the United States), boys are circumcised at puberty as a rite of passage. Today circumcision is most often performed on newborn baby boys by a doctor or a religious person trained to do it properly and safely. About half of all baby boys in the

---

[8] papules (**pap**-yools)
[9] foreskin (**fawr**-skin)
[10] circumcision (sur-kuhm-**sizh**-uhn)
[11] smegma (**smeg**-ma)

United States are circumcised. Most men in the world, however, are not circumcised.

Years ago doctors recommended circumcision for all baby boys because they believed that it prevented or cured some diseases. Some people feel that circumcision promotes cleanliness or health. Other people feel that there's no reason to perform surgery on babies.

It doesn't matter whether a man's penis is circumcised or uncircumcised. For most men, there is no effect, one way or the other, on sexual sensation.

It is not recommended that circumcision be done once a boy is in his teens. It is painful and may lead to loss of sensation. It should be done only if there is a problem with the foreskin not moving over the head normally.

Circumcised Penis

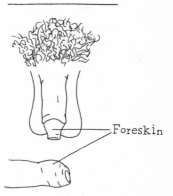

Uncircumcised Penis

Foreskin

Scrotum

The soft pouch of wrinkly skin that you see on either side and slightly behind your penis is the scrotum, which is divided inside into two pouches. Each pouch holds one testis. Many people refer to the *scrotum* and *testes* altogether as the *"testicles"* or "balls."

In adult men, usually the left side of the testicles hangs lower, and the testicle on the right is larger. This helps keep the testes from rubbing against or squishing each other while a man is walking or running.

Testes

You can feel the testes inside your scrotum. They are rather hard, sort of like a grape. You can roll them around. Testes are made up of a number of compartments, inside of which are tiny tubes, all intertwined. That is where the hormone *testosterone* is made. Testosterone helps produce sperm and also causes many of the pubertal changes to your body, such as facial hair, deepening voice, and muscle growth.

Because the sperm inside the testes are sensitive to heat, they must be kept several degrees cooler than the temperature of the body or they will die. So if the testes get too warm, the scrotum hangs farther down from the body to help cool them off. If they get too cold, muscles in the scrotum pull them

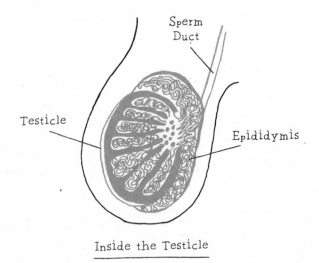

Inside the Testicle

closer to the body to warm up. This is why when a boy or man swims in cold water, he can feel his scrotum contract.

The scrotum also tightens up:

- When the penis is erect.
- If a male feels frightened or nervous. Although they're really important, the testes have nothing around them to protect them. Getting closer to the body makes them safer.

In Chapter 7, I will go into questions about penis size and other such matters.

Anus

In both females and males, the *anus*[12] is the small entrance to the *rectum* through which bowel movements (also called *feces*,[13] *stool*, or "poop") leave the body. Unlike the female body, which has three openings from front to back (the urethra, the vagina, and the anus), the male body has two openings, the one at the penile tip—the urethra—and the other at the anus.

Ejaculation

Once you begin puberty, you start making sperm. When a man is sexually excited and ready to ejaculate, the *prostate gland*[14] begins a series of rapid contractions that force the sperm

---

[12] anus (**ey**-nuhs)

[13] feces (**fee**-seez): bowel movement. Feces is made up of the food material that the body does not need, which travels into the rectum and out the anus.

[14] prostate (**pros**-teyt) gland: a male organ that acts like a muscle to release urine

from the testicles through the seminal vesicle, where it mixes with other fluids to form semen (also called "cum" or "jism" or "jiz"), a whitish fluid full of nutrients and sugar.

At different times, the semen might be any color from white to clear, and it can be thick or thin. *Ejaculation*[15] is when the muscles pump the semen down the hollow urethral tube and out the end of the penis, releasing about a teaspoon of fluid. The speed of an ejaculation can vary from dribbling to shooting out semen really fast. All of this is normal. But no matter how it comes out, semen is always filled with 300 to 500 million sperm, any one of which can make a female pregnant if intercourse occurs. By the way, an *erection*[16] can (but doesn't have to) end with ejaculation. Most boys have their first experience of ejaculation while *masturbating* (rubbing, pulling, or stroking the penis and making it stiff) or having a wet dream. I explain more about masturbation in Chapter 10.

Pre-ejaculate is a fluid that oozes out of the penis before ejaculation. It does not contain sperm on its own but it may include a small amount of sperm if a previous ejaculation has occurred recently. This means that, with sexual intercourse, pregnancy can sometimes result from pre-ejaculate fluid.

---

during urination and helps pump sperm from the testicles through the seminal vesicle in preparation for ejaculation.

[15] ejaculation (ih-jak-yuh-**ley**-shuhn): the process by which semen is pumped down the hollow urethral tube and released out the end of the penis; also known as a male orgasm.

[16] erection (ih-**rek**-shuhn): the process by which the penis becomes erect or hard. During an erection a lot of blood is carried into your penis through the blood vessels, and it fills the empty spaces of the spongy erectile tissue, which swells up and presses against the blood vessels, causing the blood to remain in the penis.

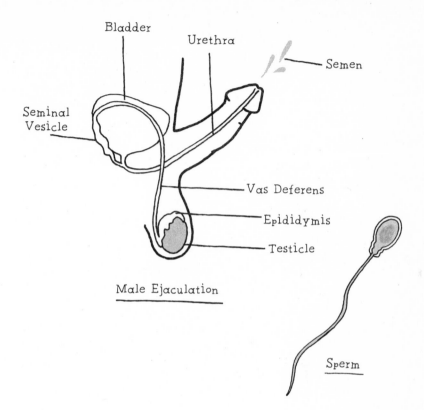

Bladder

Urethra

Semen

Seminal
Vesicle

Vas Deferens

Epididymis

Testicle

Male Ejaculation

Sperm

Sexual Intercourse and Conception

Sexual intercourse is how a man and a woman can make a baby. It can be a beautiful, exciting, loving act that gives pleasure to both partners, even if they are not planning to make a baby.

This is how sexual intercourse can lead to conception: The man's erect penis goes inside the woman's *vagina*, which, if the woman is excited enough, has become lubricated and more

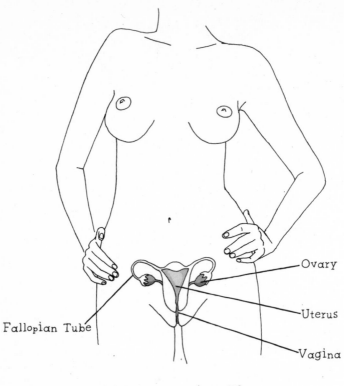

Interior Sex Organs in a Woman

slippery, allowing the penis to slide in easily. After a period of lovemaking, during which the penis moves in and out of the vagina, the man ejaculates, sending millions of sperm swimming up the vagina and into the uterus. If just one of those millions of sperm connects with the woman's *ovum,* or egg, a baby begins to grow.

A girl is born with all of her eggs. Once a month, in an adult woman, an egg leaves the ovary and goes into the fallopian tube.

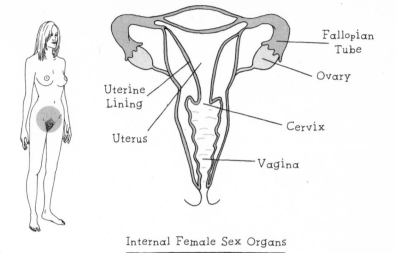

Internal Female Sex Organs

This process is called *ovulation*.[17] The ripe egg is swept down the tube by tiny hairs as it heads for the uterus. If a sperm has reached the uterus and enters the egg within twenty-four hours of when the egg left the ovary, *fertilization*[18] takes place, the egg becomes planted in the uterus, and a fetus will begin to grow.

If the egg is not fertilized, it breaks down and flows out of the woman's body, together with blood and tissue. This is called *menstruation*[19] or "having a period."

---

[17] ovulation (ov-yuh-**ley**-shun)

[18] fertilization (fur-tl-uh-**zey**-shuhn): the union of the woman's egg with the man's sperm.

[19] menstruation (men-stroo-**ey**-shuhn): the process by which a woman's unfertilized egg breaks down and flows out of the woman's body, together with blood and tissue. Menstruation happens to women about once a month for the years after puberty until menopause. It is commonly known

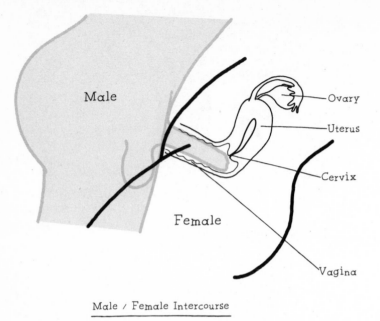

Male / Female Intercourse

Reasons to See a Doctor

Here are some reasons you'd need to ask a grown-up to make
an appointment for you with a doctor:

- You're eight and a half to nine years old and have already started puberty, or you're fourteen to fifteen
  and haven't experienced any hormonal changes such
  as acne, a growth spurt, pubic hair, or body odor.
- You can't fully retract your foreskin (the skin covering the end of your penis, for those not circumcised), and it causes pain or discomfort.

---

as "having a period." On average, *menopause* happens between ages forty-five
and fifty-one. After menopause, a woman ceases having periods and cannot
produce eggs to create a baby.

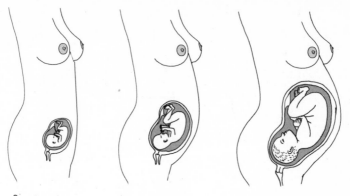

3 Months   6 Months   9 Months

Pregnancy

- You injure one or both testes. This will hurt a lot, but wait an hour or so. If the pain continues or if you become swollen or bruised, you need to be checked.
- You have a sore (painful or not), tender spot, blister, rash, or wart anywhere on your genitals that doesn't go away in a day or two.
- You have a scaly, itchy rash. First buy an antifungal cream, which can prevent or cure fungus. If it doesn't clear up, you need to be checked.
- You feel pain anywhere in your genitals or lower abdomen. Sudden, severe pain in your testicles, especially with blood in your urine or nausea, is a potential emergency and requires an emergency doctor visit.

- You have a painful erection, not caused by sexual stimulation, for four hours or more. This is called priapism and is an emergency.
- You feel a lump anywhere in or on your genitals.
- You have any kind of unusual discharge coming out of your penis.
- You see any kind of change in your urine.
- You feel burning or pain when you urinate or have to do it often.
- You have a bad smell under your foreskin.
- You have persistent redness on your face from shaving irritation or cuts, or you have infected in-grown hairs.
- You're bothered by persistent questions or concerns about your body.

Each time you have a checkup, the doctor should examine your testicles. Don't be embarrassed! Doctors examine testes all the time, and it's so common for the examination to cause an erection that the doctor won't pay any attention. He or she will be focused on much more important things!

5.

Girls' Sexual and Reproductive Parts and How They Function

Hormones

As with boys, puberty[1] in girls is caused by hormones. Hormones are made by different *glands* in your body that are part of its *endocrine system*.[2] A gland is a group of cells that produces chemicals and hormones. Hormones act as messengers that travel through the bloodstream from these glands. Different

[1] puberty (**pyoo**-ber-tee): the biological part of the early adolescent years when the sexual and reproductive systems start to mature
[2] endocrine (**en**-duh-krin) system: controls the body's hormone functions and makes sure they run together smoothly

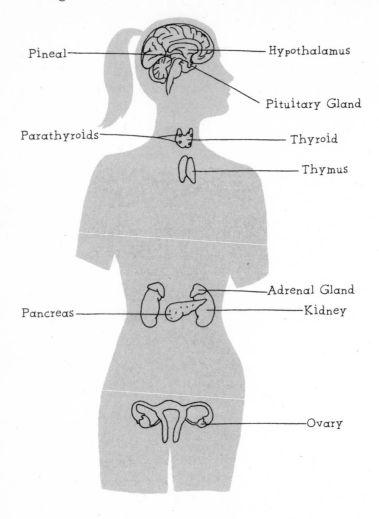

Pineal

Hypothalamus

Pituitary Gland

Parathyroids

Thyroid

Thymus

Adrenal Gland

Pancreas

Kidney

Ovary

Female Endocrine System

hormones go to different glands and tell them what to do. By raising and lowering the levels of various hormones at different times, the endocrine system controls the body's functions and makes sure that they run together smoothly.

The body has many kinds of hormones. The two most important sex hormones, *testosterone* and *estrogen,* are produced by both males and females, but, starting at puberty, girls make much more estrogen and boys make much more testosterone.

Becoming Familiar with Yourself

Get a hand mirror and sit somewhere (on the floor or a chair) where you can pull your knees up and position yourself so that you can see a reflection of your vulva, clitoris, and vagina without casting a shadow. Use the hand that's not holding the

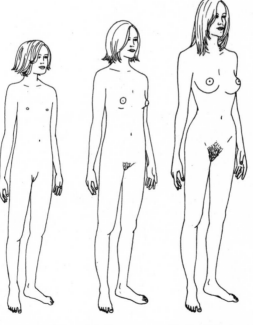

Prepubertal   Adolescent   Fully Matured

mirror to separate the folds of your labia and try to identify the different parts. If you do this, I want you to remember that you won't look exactly like any picture you might have seen. It is normal for everyone to be different. Your finger-nails and toes don't look exactly like anyone else's, and nei-ther do your genitals. Some women have very long, thick labia, and some have very thin, small labia. This is all nor-mal. Like the rest of your body, the genitals grow and change during puberty.

Female Genitals

Some girls may have been taught that it is wrong to look at their genitals or to touch them except when using the toilet. I think it is a good idea to look at your genitals. I think it's important to know what you look like, what the different parts are, and what they are for. It's important to look at your genitals now, while you are young. How will you know what "not right" is if you don't know what "normal" is?

Mons or Pubis
Your genitals are protected by a raised mound of flesh over your pubic bone that is called the *pubis* or *mons.*[3] You may have some hair, called *pubic hair,* over your mons. As you grow, the hair will become thicker, darker, and curlier, and the mons will thicken and may stick out more.

---

[3]   pubis (**pyoo**-bis) or mons (monz)

Farther down between your legs is the *vulva,* the external genitals.

Vulva

Inside the vulva are two sets of soft folded skin, one inside the other, called the *labia.*[4] This is the Latin word for "lips." Labia vary in color from pale pink to brownish black, depending largely on your race, ethnicity, and age. Most older women's labia become darker.

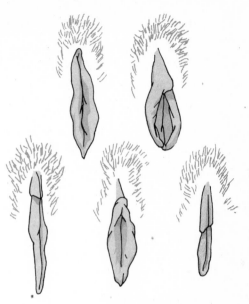

Vaginal lips can look a variety of ways.

The medical name for the outer labia is the *labia majora.*[5] In younger girls, the outer labia are flat and hairless and do not come together. During puberty, these labia grow some pubic hair and thicken so that they do come together.

During childhood the undersides of the outer labia are smooth, but during puberty they can develop small bumps. These are glands that begin to produce a small amount of oil during puberty to moisten the area so that it does not get irritated. The outer labia also have sweat glands.

If you separate the outer labia, you will see the inner labia

---

[4] labia (**lay**-bee-uh)
[5] labia majora (ma-**jor**-uh)

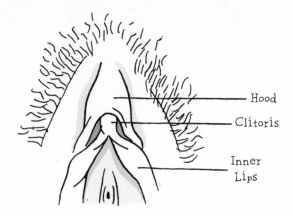

Hood

Clitoris

Inner
Lips

or *labia minora.*[6] These are small and not well defined until puberty, when they, too, can become plumper. In fact, in some women, the inner labia come out farther than the outer ones, or one is larger than the other. Although they don't grow hair like the outer labia, they, too, have oil glands.

Both pairs of labia cover and protect the inner parts of the vulva, which are the *clitoris*[7] and the two openings to the *urethra*[8] and the *vagina.*[9] During puberty these openings, which start out small, grow larger and become easier to see.

Clitoris

At the top of the vulva—that part closest to the front of your body, where the inner lips meet—is the clitoris, the tip of which is a small mound of very sensitive tissue about the size

[6] labia minora (mi-**nor**-uh)
[7] clitoris (**klit**-er-is)
[8] urethra (yoo-**ree**-thruh)
[9] vagina (vuh-**ji**-nuh)

of a pea or a pencil eraser that grows larger during puberty. It is protected by the *clitoral hood,* a fold of skin that covers it and that you may have to pull up in order to see it. What you are actually looking at is the tip of the clitoris, which has a shaft that extends into the body. If you press down above the clitoris, you may be able to feel this shaft, which in adult women is about four inches long.

The clitoris is full of nerve endings that make it very sensitive, like a boy's penis. Touching and rubbing the clitoris can make a girl or woman feel good throughout her genital and reproductive area. It is her main source of sexual pleasure and orgasm, the wonderful release of sexual tension that can follow sexual arousal. Whereas a penis is a multitasker, used for peeing, sexual intercourse, and making babies, the clitoris's only purpose is for pleasure!

Urethra

The first opening below the clitoris is to the urethra. The urethra is not a sex organ, but the tube that carries urine from the *bladder,* where it is stored, out of the body. Urine[10] is the liquid waste left over from food and drink that the body does not use. In females urine is the only fluid that travels through this tube. It may look like an upside down *V* with tiny slits on either side of it. The slits are the openings for tiny glands that make fluid to keep the area moist.

---

[10] urine (**yoor**-in)

Vagina

The second opening is to the vagina. The vagina is a stretchy, muscular passageway that connects the uterus—a sexual and reproductive organ inside the female body—to the outside. During puberty, it nearly doubles in length until it is three to five inches long.

Although the muscular walls of the vagina keep it closed most of the time, they also stretch. Like a balloon, the vagina can enlarge enormously during childbirth. During sexual intercourse, the male penis fits into the vagina, and when a baby is born, the flexible vaginal muscles help push it out.

At times two different fluids come out of the vagina. One is a daily discharge that cleans it, and the other is the mixture of blood and tissue that leaves the female body monthly during menstruation.[11]

Hymen

The vaginal opening may be partly covered by a piece of skin called the *hymen*.[12] In young girls, it is very thin, and during puberty it becomes thicker and can develop ruffles and folds. Otherwise it's hard to describe what it looks like. The reason is that the hymen naturally stretches and tears when you are very active, such as playing sports or riding horses or bikes, when you explore your vagina with your finger, or when, during

[11] menstruation (men-stroo-ey-shun): the process by which a woman's unfertilized egg breaks down and flows out of the woman's body, together with blood and tissue. Menstruation happens to women about once a month for the years after puberty until menopause. It is commonly known as "having a period." On average, *menopause* occurs between ages forty-five and fifty-one. After menopause, a woman ceases having periods and cannot produce eggs to create a baby.
[12] hymen (hay-muhn)

your period, you use a tampon. Your hymen can have a few large openings or several smaller ones.

Today, because girls tend to be very active, the hymen has usually torn before they have sexual intercourse. In some cultures around the world, a girl must have an intact hymen to prove her virginity. The hymen is then broken during intercourse (when the penis enters the vagina). These days, certainly in the United States, a girl's virginity is not determined by her having an intact hymen. As I said, it is too common for the hymen to stretch due to normal activity for that to be a reliable indicator of virginity.

Sometimes parents will bring a girl to the doctor asking if she is a virgin. In many cultures, even today in the United States, parents believe a doctor can tell if a girl is a virgin or not. This is not possible! No doctor should tell you that a physical exam can determine whether you are a virgin.

When your hymen stretches, you may not feel anything, or you may feel some soreness or have a little bleeding. All of the hymen may finally go away, or a fringe of tissue may be left around the edges of the vaginal opening.

Anus

Farther back behind the vagina is the *anus*,[13] the small entrance to the *rectum* through which bowel movements (also called *feces*,[14] or *stool* or "poop") leave the body. In both males and females, the food material that the body does not need travels into the rectum and out the anus as a bowel movement.

---

[13] anus (**ey-nuhs**)
[14] feces (**fee-seez**)

During puberty the skin around the anus may darken, and you may get some pubic hair growing there. But the anus isn't part of the vulva—it's just very close to it. To avoid getting an infection in your vagina, after you have a bowel movement, reach around behind you and wipe yourself from front to back.

The Internal Reproductive Organs

The major reproductive organs inside the female body are two *ovaries*,[15] two *Fallopian tubes*,[16] the *uterus*[17] with its *cervix*,[18] and the vagina. As you read the following descriptions, look at the picture, which shows how these organs look after puberty.

Ovaries

On each side above the uterus is an ovary. Each is the shape of a large almond. The ovaries contain a female's sex cells. These cells are also called "eggs," or the Latin word *ova*—one cell is called an *ovum*.[19]

[15] ovaries (**oh**-vuh-rees)
[16] Fallopian tubes: the passageways through which the woman's egg travels from the ovaries to the uterus
[17] uterus (**yoo**-ter-uhs): Sometimes called the womb, the uterus is the organ in a woman where the fetus grows.
[18] cervix (**sur**-viks): the "neck" or the bottom of the uterus that sits at the top of the vagina
[19] ova [plural] (**oh**-vuh) or ovum [singular] (**oh**-vuhm)

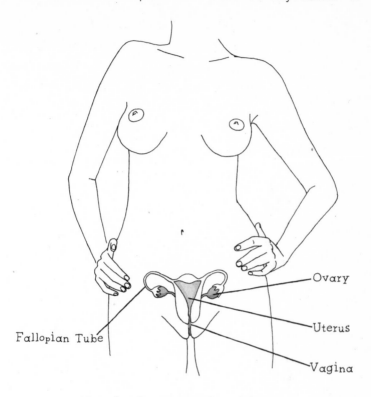

Interior Sex Organs in a Woman

Ova (Eggs)

The ovaries of each baby girl contain one to two million egg cells, but they are not yet fertile—that is, able to produce babies. When the girl reaches puberty, she has between 300,000 and 400,000 egg cells that are mature enough to become babies.

Usually an adult woman makes a ripe *ovum* (one egg) one time each month. The egg develops in one of her ovaries, and

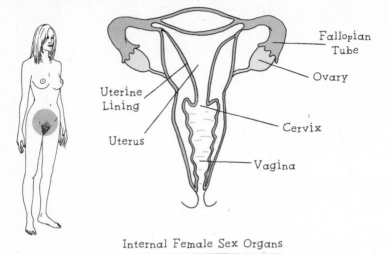

Internal Female Sex Organs

when it is mature, it will leave the ovary and go into the Fallopian or uterine tube. This process is called *ovulation*.[20]

Fallopian Tubes
The Fallopian tubes are named after Gabriele Falloppio, the Italian scientist who discovered them. Each tube is three to four inches long and about the diameter of a spaghetti strand. One end drapes over each ovary, and because of their shape, Falloppio called them "the trumpets of the uterus." The ends have *fimbriae,* which is Latin for "fringes." The fimbriae, which look like tentacles or feathers, connect the ovaries to the uterus.

The fallopian tubes are the passageways through which eggs travel from the ovaries to the uterus. The tubes are lined with tiny hairs called *cilia,* which means "eyelashes." The cilia wave back and forth to move the eggs along to the uterus.

[20] ovulation (ov-yuh-**ley**-shun)

Uterus

The uterus is sometimes called the womb. Inside the uterus is a lining called the *endometrium*,[21] which you'll learn more about in Chapter 9.

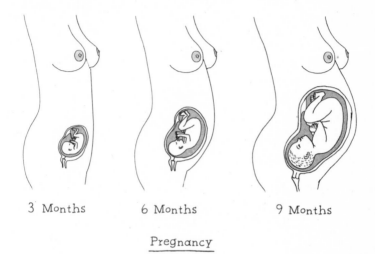

3 Months   6 Months   9 Months

Pregnancy

The fertilized egg lives in this cushionlike endometrial lining and receives food for about nine months as it develops into a fetus and then a baby. As the fetus grows, the uterus stretches and makes the mother's belly look big. After the mother gives birth, the uterus shrinks back to its usual size, which is about the size of your fist.

Cervix

The cervix, or "neck," is the narrow bottom of the uterus that sits at the top of the vagina. The cervix normally has a very small opening, about the size of the tip of a pencil. During

---

[21] endometrium (en-doh-**mee**-tree-uhm)

childbirth, the cervix begins to dilate (or open) when it is time for the baby to be born. When the uterus begins to contract and the mother pushes the baby out, the cervix stretches from the size of the tip of a pencil to about four or five inches across.

Menstruation

If, however, an egg is not fertilized, it breaks down and flows out of the woman's vagina together with blood and tissue. This is called menstruation or "having a period." (More about menstruation in Chapter 9)

Sexual Intercourse and Conception

Sexual intercourse is how a man and a woman can make a baby. It can be a beautiful, exciting, loving act that gives pleasure to both partners, even if they are not planning to make a baby.

This is how sexual intercourse can lead to conception: The man's erect penis goes inside the woman's vagina, which, if she is excited enough, has become lubricated and more slippery, allowing the penis to slide in easily. After a period of lovemaking, during which the penis moves in and out of the vagina, the man ejaculates, sending millions of sperm swimming up the vagina and into the uterus.

If one of those sperm reaches the uterus and enters the egg within twenty-four hours of when the egg left the ovary, *fertilization* takes place, the egg becomes planted in the uterus, and a baby will begin to grow.

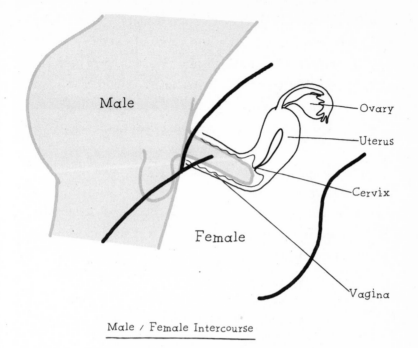

Male / Female Intercourse

Reasons to See a Doctor

- You are seven or younger and have started puberty. Young girls may have pubic hair or hair in their armpits. It may be normal, depending on when the other women in your family started puberty, but it's best to ask to see your doctor to have it checked out. Breast development before age eight is considered too early.
- You have no signs of puberty by thirteen or fourteen, or you have not started a period within two years of starting breast development.

- Your periods are very heavy or prolonged. Most teens use four to five pads or tampons per day during the first few days of their period, and fewer pads or tampons afterwards. If you are using more than that, or if you are bleeding with clots, you may have a bleeding disorder that requires treatment. Heavy periods can be the first sign of a bleeding disorder.
- Your periods are not regular within six months of starting to menstruate.
- You have very painful periods, which cause you to miss school or activities, or are associated with vomiting.
- You are unable to insert a tampon.
- You have vaginal discharge (fluid from the vagina) that smells bad, is itchy, thick, or green or yellow.
- You have painful blisters, lumps or bumps, rashes, or growths on your genitals.
- You have pain with urination or with intercourse.
- You have blood in your urine when you do not have your period.
- You have firm or painful lumps in your breasts.
- You have breasts that are different sizes, or your breasts are so large that they cause back pain or prevent you from engaging in physical activity.
- You have a sudden onset of fever, a red rash, vomiting, headache, or confusion during your period. These could indicate Toxic Shock Syndrome and require an immediate visit to a medical provider.
- You are bothered by any persistent questions or concerns about your body.

6.

Changes in Both Girls and Boys That You Can See

As your hormones increase, the first signs of puberty can include changes in your skin, your voice, and your smell, and a sudden growth spurt that makes you taller. Perhaps you've already experienced this, or are experiencing it now. Feel free to skip those categories that don't apply to you.

Growth Spurt

The growth spurt that you have during puberty starts with your feet, then your arms and legs, and finally the rest of you. So don't be surprised if at first you start tripping over yourself!

As time passes, your muscles thicken, and you grow stronger. Boys' shoulders get broader.

Growing Pains

Growing pains usually occur in younger children rather than teenagers, but they may occur in early puberty. They occur in the long bones of the legs, so they are felt in the thighs or the calves. They generally occur in late afternoon or evening, and they may even wake you from sleep. A hot-water bottle or a massage may help. Growing pains do not occur in the knees or ankles, and they should not cause you to limp or stop going to school or playing sports.

If you are still experiencing growing pains, try applying a hot-water bottle or heating pad to where it hurts, or do something aerobic, such as taking a brisk walk, riding a bike, swimming, or anything else that gets your heart going. Or try a pain-relief medicine from the drugstore. Ibuprofen (Midol, Advil, and Motrin) and Aleve are some that can be effective.

Skin

Acne
Many teenagers get pimples on their skin, also known as *acne*. This usually goes away by the end of your teen years if not sooner, though some people have acne into adulthood.

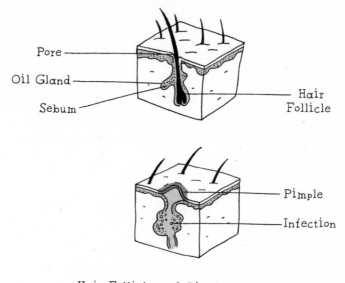

Pore

Oil Gland

Sebum

Hair Follicle

Pimple

Infection

Hair Follicle and Pimple Anatomy

Acne happens because the oil glands, which are right under the skin, are becoming more active, producing more oil than usual. This causes three types of acne: whiteheads, blackheads, and pimples.

In the case of *whiteheads,* the pores in your skin on your face, chest, or back get blocked by *sebum,* a substance made by the oil glands. The sebum can't get out, and this creates a white bump.

If the bump pushes outward, a chemical reaction on the skin turns it dark. We call these *blackheads.*

Pimples are caused when bacteria on the surface of the skin become trapped inside the pore blocked with sebum and become infected. If the infection inside the pore erupts and spreads, it causes redness and large bumps.

Here are some things you can do to reduce the appearance of acne:

- Wash your face twice a day with mild soap and water to clear away the oiliness.
- Do not pop or pick the pimples. This only spreads the pus (bacteria) and can leave scars.
- If basic skin care doesn't improve your acne, consult your doctor. Most family doctors are quite comfortable with acne care. If your acne is more severe and requires special medicines that only a dermatologist can prescribe, your doctor will help you find one. Your doctor (or a medical clinic, if you don't have a doctor) should be able to recommend such a person to you or your parents.

One important ingredient to look for in an acne-treatment cream is salicylic acid. Tetracycline can also be effective but it requires a prescription.

Some scrubs, cleansers, or mail-order products don't work well and are expensive. Avoid abrasive soaps and harsh products that can dry out your skin, causing you to produce even more oil. Basic face cleansers are always best.

Sun Damage

Darkly pigmented people, or those who don't burn, can still experience sun damage. A few sunburns early in life are associated with skin cancers later on and contribute to faster aging and wrinkles.

Everyone should use sunscreen. Wear a sunscreen with an SPF of 30 or more every day, including when it's cloudy. Apply more every couple of hours if you are at the beach, or if you go in for a swim or are sweating a lot. Many face creams now include sunblock; get one that does.

The ultraviolet rays of tanning beds damage skin in the same way the sun does. Any change in skin color, from a tanning bed or from the sun directly, is a sign of sun damage. Avoid tanning beds. Spray tans are not great for your skin, either.

Body Odor

Like your oil glands, your sweat glands become more active during your teen years, leading to increased body odor under your arms, around the genitals, and on the hands and feet, especially when you're nervous or excited.

You may already be wearing deodorant or antiperspirant every day. A word about that. Deodorant is designed to improve the smell of your body, while antiperspirant is designed to reduce the amount of sweat you actually secrete.

Other than using antiperspirant or deodorant, here are some things you can do to reduce body odor:

- Shower or bathe daily.
- Wear clean clothes. Dirty clothes trap bacteria that smell.
- Wear cotton clothing. It allows air to circulate more freely than other fabrics, like polyester and silk.

Now we'll discuss the physical changes that are unique to boys.

7.

Changes in Boys' Bodies
That You Can See

How Hormones Work

Not everyone's body changes at the same time and in the same ways during adolescence. This is because each person's body produces hormones at a different rate. Some boys will develop and become more physically mature earlier than others. Everyone will have a mature body sooner or later.

Penis Size

- Penis size has nothing to do with body size.
- You cannot tell from a soft penis how large it will be when it is erect. Some penises are very small when soft and very large when erect. Some penises don't change size very much between the soft and erect stage. Being nervous, scared, or cold can cause your scrotum to pull up your testes for safety, and your soft penis can shrink up to two inches! Being relaxed or warm can make a soft penis look twice as large.
- Although soft penises vary a lot in size from male to male, the average erect adult penis is between five and seven inches. But the size of your erection changes a little from time to time also, depending on the exact situation you're in when you have one.
- Having a larger penis does not make you more masculine, more sexual, or better at having sex.

Most women's pleasure during intercourse comes from the stimulation she receives on and around the clitoris, which is outside the vagina, and in the first few inches of the inside of her vagina. In addition, the level of a woman's pleasure is affected by her emotional connection to her partner, more than the size of his penis.

Erections

Now that your body is producing a lot of the hormone called testosterone, your penis is more sensitive, causing more frequent erections, sometimes at inconvenient times. Erections happen when you become aroused, causing the vessels in the penis to fill with blood.

Erections can happen very fast, from totally soft to really hard in seconds. They can also happen more slowly. They can be hard as a bone (hence the term "boner," even though there is no bone in the penis) or less hard. With stimulation, erections can last for hours . . . or not. An erect penis can stick straight out at a right angle to your body, or it can stick upward, closer to your stomach, or it can curve—usually to the left. All of these variables are normal.

With an erection, the blood vessels along the shaft are easier to see. The glans, or head, may get darker. The testicles may become tighter and closer to your body. Again, it is all normal.

Spontaneous Erections

During adolescence, boys can have totally unexpected erections. These are called spontaneous erections and they can be embarrassing, such as when you're walking down the street and see someone you find attractive. Erections can happen for no reason at all! Just keep in mind that they aren't as noticeable to others as you think they are. A spontaneous erection that does not soften after four hours, or is painful, requires medical attention.

Here are some suggestions for how to stop or disguise an erection:

- If the erection is caused by thoughts or feelings, try to relax and think about something else. Count backward by 3's.
- Put your hands into your pockets and push your pants forward. It helps if you are wearing baggy pants.
- Sit down. If you can't sit behind a table or desk, try crossing one leg over the other.
- Hold a book, notebook, or papers in front of you.
- Move behind a piece of furniture.
- Tie a sweater or sweatshirt around your waist.
- Wear long shirts that can hang outside your pants.

Most erections will just go away unless there is stimulation.

Wet Dreams

As you know by now, males often wake up with erections. This happens when the bladder fills with urine during the night. The pressure from the bulging bladder can stimulate nerves at the base of the penis, causing it to become erect. You may find that you've ejaculated during the night in your sleep. The scientific name for this type of ejaculation, *nocturnal emission*, means "nighttime release." It's not really accurate, because it can occur anytime that you're asleep. The usual name for it, "wet dream," isn't really accurate, either, because you can ejaculate without dreaming.

Either way, you'll wake up with sticky semen on your body, pajamas, or bedsheets. If it has dried, it may look like a thin yellowish paste.

Although not everyone has wet dreams, after puberty many males do have them.

Taking Care of Yourself

Because your genitals are outside your body, they require extra attention. Wash your genitals with soap and water, cleaning all the skin folds, every day. Dry thoroughly to avoid getting a fungus, which causes an itchy rash. Fungal infections are very common and can usually be cleared up by "jock itch" products sold in drugstores.

Dry cotton underpants that feel soft to your skin and aren't too tight are a good idea. Cotton is important because it allows your genitals to breathe and, unlike synthetic fabrics, doesn't trap bacteria in the genital area.

Athletic Supporters

Boys who play sports often wear athletic supporters, which are also called jockstraps. These are special covers for the penis and scrotum.

For sports like running, some athletic supporters fit like snug jockey shorts and either press your genitals against your body or support them in a sling lining or in soft cups. Others are held in place by actual straps. For some sports, like football, baseball, basketball, and hockey, athletic programs require jockstraps with hard cups.

You can find athletic supporters in the boys' and men's clothing sections and sports sections of department stores, in sporting goods stores, and in some drugstores. To buy one, all you need to know is the size of your waist. Just look on the label for the correct size in inches. Some brands have cups in two sizes, youth and adult.

Like your underwear, your jockstrap should fit as comfortably as possible, without chafing, and should always be kept clean. It's a good idea to have more than one so that you always have a clean one when you need it.

Other External Signs of Puberty

Okay, we talked about the penis and all its parts and behaviors. Now we'll discuss the other changes boys experience during puberty and adolescence due to the increase in hormone production.

Voice Changes
Your voice may well have changed and deepened already. Your larynx, which produces your deeper voice, may now have begun to stick out from the front of your neck in a bump called an Adam's apple.

Hair Growth
After your voice changes, your beard may start to grow, usually very slowly for the first few years. Your hair changes, too.

It increases and darkens on your legs, grows under your arms (where you may have more sweat and body odor), and may appear also on your chest, back, abdomen, or shoulders.

The pubic hair around the base of the penis becomes curlier, then turns coarser and darker. As the hair takes on the

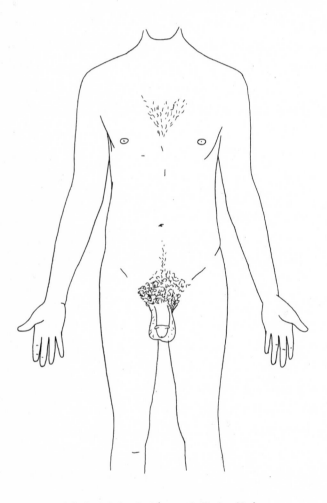

Adult Male Pubic and Body Hair

color and texture seen in grown men, it starts to form an upside-down triangle.

How much hair a man will have depends on traits inherited from his parents and his ethnic background. Having a lot or almost no hair does not make you more or less masculine.

Facial Hair

Facial hair usually appears on boys at age fourteen or fifteen. Some people might tell you that shaving right away will make your hair come in thicker. That is a myth.

For many boys, starting to shave every day is a big decision. Whether you want to start shaving is entirely up to you. On average, a boy starts shaving sometime between eleven and seventeen years.

If you have curly hair, it might be a good idea to have someone, perhaps a relative or a barber, teach you the best way for you to shave without irritating your face. There are shaving gels made especially for various skin types and ethnicities.

Breasts

As your testosterone levels adjust and settle down, you might develop *gynecomastia.*[1] This temporary condition causes your breasts to enlarge and become tender or sore. Your nipples can also enlarge and darken, and you may develop a flat bump that looks like a button under one or both of them. Don't worry! Gynecomastia occurs in more than half of teenage boys as they go through puberty. It is more common in boys who are overweight or who use a lot of marijuana. Consult your family

---

[1]   gynecomastia (guy-nuh-co-**mast**-ia)

doctor if the breast tissue is very firm, painful, has any liquid coming from the nipple, or lasts longer than a few months.

All these changes don't always happen in exactly the same way, at the same time, for everyone. Depending on what the hormones in your body decide, you may start puberty by developing pubic hair, or underarm hair, or both at the same time.

8.

Changes in Girls' Bodies
That You Can See

Weight Gain

During puberty it is normal not only to grow taller but also to gain weight. This stage lasts about three years, and a girl may gain between thirty-five and fifty-five pounds during this time. Instead of dieting, eat healthily (see page 211 in Chapter 19) and stay physically active.

Breasts

Each breast has a raised nipple, surrounded by a circle of skin of the same color called the *areola*.[1] The breasts themselves are made of fat tissue, milk glands, and ducts. After a woman has a baby, the glands will produce milk, which then travels through the ducts to the nipples, each of which has several tiny openings through which the baby can suck the milk.

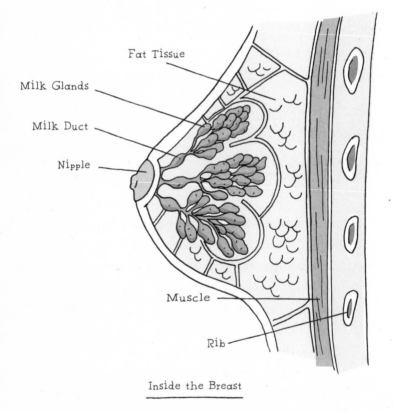

Fat Tissue

Milk Glands

Milk Duct

Nipple

Muscle

Rib

Inside the Breast

[1]   areola (uh-**ree**-uh-luh)

Sometimes when a nipple is squeezed, a discharge comes out that may look white, clear, or pale yellow-green. Or you may see a little crust around a nipple where fluid came out and dried. Now and then the body makes this fluid to wash out the breast ducts. This is normal.

The nipples and areolae vary in color from light pink to dark brown. Some are quite small and others can be very large, covering almost the entire end of the breast. Nipples are very sensitive and may respond to cold, touch, or sexual feelings by becoming erect. The nipples stiffen and stand up, and the areolae may tighten up and look bumpy. After a while, the nipples return to normal.

Breast Development

Doctors divide breast growth into five stages.
- **Stage 1: Childhood.** During childhood, breasts are flat. The nipple sticks out from a small areola.
- **Stage 2: Breast Buds.** When puberty begins, breast buds develop. These are raised bumps that start to grow under the nipples. This is normal. Both the nipples and the areolae grow larger and darker. It's normal sometimes to feel a little tenderness or itchiness in your breasts. This stage can last from several months to over a year.
- **Stage 3: Development.** As the nipples and areolae keep growing and getting darker, breasts, too, grow larger and may look a little pointed. This stage also can last from a few months to a few years.

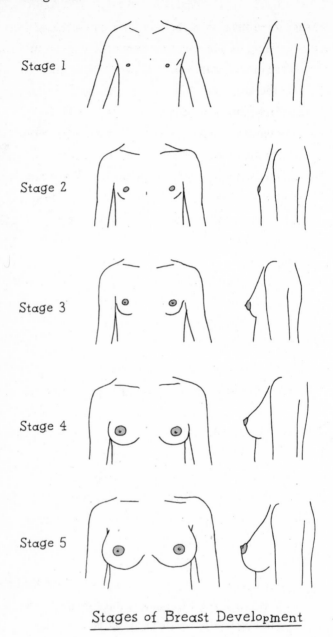

Stage 1

Stage 2

Stage 3

Stage 4

Stage 5

Stages of Breast Development

- **Stage 4: Mound.** You may see the nipple and are-ola blending into a separate mound that sticks out from the breast. It may not happen, or it may happen in the next stage.
- **Stage 5: Adulthood.** Breasts develop completely, usually with a full, round shape. The areola blends into each breast and may develop a few hairs around its edges. Usually the nipple rises above it, but some women instead have inverted nipples— nipples that go inward.

If inverted nipples develop during puberty, they are nor-mal, and when you have a baby you can breast-feed normally,

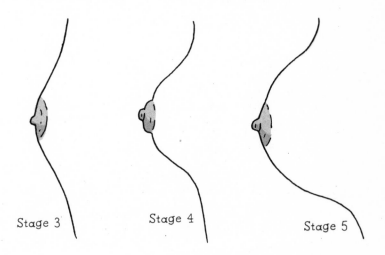

Stage 3

Stage 4

Stage 5

In Stage 4, the nipple sticks out from the breast with its own little mound.

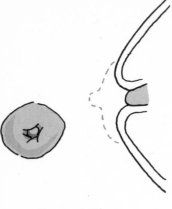

Inverted Nipple

so learn how to clean them. You can ask a doctor or medical clinic what to do.

One breast may begin to get larger than the other. Very often, breasts will not grow to be exactly alike—one may be shaped a little differently or hang a little lower. This is normal, just as it's normal for your hands or eyes or other pairs of body parts each to look a little different.

Remember that nobody can really predict exactly how your breasts will grow, how long it will take, or how large they will get. Breasts come in all sizes, shapes, and coloration. Girls often worry that their breasts are too small. Large breasts can attract teasing.

Don't be fooled by any person or advertisement claiming that your breasts can be made bigger by doing certain exercises or by rubbing in creams or taking any pills or potions. No product like that can change your breasts.

Learn how to do a breast self-exam every month after your period. This is a great habit to get into as you approach adulthood. If you are concerned about the asymmetry of your breasts, or the size causes you pain, or you have noticed a new lump or bump, consult your doctor.

Bras

It's easy to decide whether you want or need a bra. Try one on and ask yourself if you feel more comfortable with one or

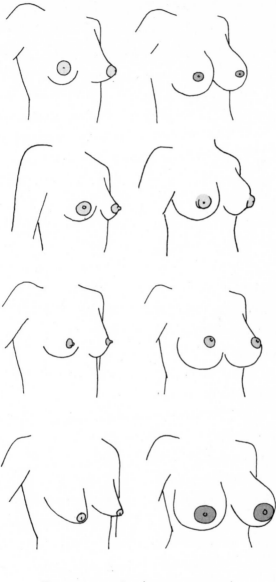

Breasts and nipples come in
all shapes and sizes.

without one. Get a training bra, one for small chests, or a sports bra, if you like, to see if you like having one.

Bra sizes have both a number and a letter, such as 34B. The number is the band size and is based on the measurement around your rib cage below your breasts. The letter is the cup size and is based on the size of your breasts measured around your chest over your nipples. Usually stores have specially trained saleswomen who can measure you accurately to get the correct size and help you try on bras. They can also consult with you on the fit.

Sizes may actually vary a little from bra to bra. Usually you can adjust the bra fit by making the straps longer or shorter. Try on several bras to find the best fit.

Bras come in all kinds of colors, fabrics, and styles:

- If you have large breasts, you might want an underwire bra for greater support.
- Girls and women with smaller breasts might like comfortable stretch bras, soft-cup bras, or padded bras.
- Special bras, like demi-bras or strapless bras, can shape the breasts for the best look under particular kinds of clothes.
- Whatever size breasts you have, get a sports bra if you play a lot of sports or just prefer the way it feels. This type of bra holds your breasts in place more securely, either by pressing them against your chest or by supporting each one in a separate cup.

Maybe you don't want to wear a bra but feel self-conscious about your decision. Your nipples might show under a thin top, or maybe you feel different because all of your girlfriends wear bras. But there are other ways to feel comfortable, like wearing a camisole or tank top under a shirt or sweater so that no one can tell that you're not wearing a bra.

Body Hair

During puberty, you begin to grow hair under your arms, on your legs, and maybe in other places on your body as well, especially over your pubic bone. The hair on your pubic bone

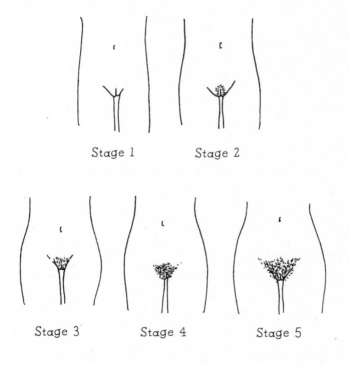

Stage 1   Stage 2

Stage 3   Stage 4   Stage 5

Stages of Pubic Hair Growth in Women

is called *pubic hair*. At first you see only a few hairs, then, as more grow, they become darker, curlier, and finally wiry. As it thickens, the pubic hair forms an upside-down triangle on your mons. The hair may grow out a little onto your thighs and up toward your belly. And it might not be the same color as the hair on your head! Some women have a lot of dark curly pubic hair while some have less hair and it may be straighter.

There is no reason to shave pubic hair, or hair under your arms or on your legs, if you don't want to.

Vaginal Discharge

As you enter puberty, you may notice a watery discharge from your vagina. This is called *leukorrhea*.[2] It can be clear and slippery at some times and white and creamy at others, and it may look a little yellow if it dries on your underpants. The discharge can have a slight odor, and if you have been sweating a lot, it can smell a little musky until you bathe.

Leukorrhea is your body's way of cleaning your vagina, the surface of which develops cells during puberty that are flushed away each day. In fact, your vagina is one of the cleanest places in your body because it cleanses itself constantly. Like the tears that you always have in your eyes, this fluid moistens your vagina and helps protect it against infections.

[2] leukorrhea (leu-kor-**rhe**-a)

Vaginal Infections

At any age you can develop a vaginal infection that will cause a different kind of discharge. An infection can cause one or more of these symptoms:

- a discharge that is thick, chunky white, or any discharge that is green or dark yellow or brown
- a discharge that is intensely itchy
- a strong smell from your vagina even after you have washed
- unusual redness on your vaginal opening or your inner labia
- burning or pain when you wash or urinate

These infections are very common and familiar to doctors, and they're usually easy to treat.

Bladder and Urinary Tract Infections (UTIs)

If you have to urinate often, feel burning when you do, or see blood in your urine, you need to take antibiotics. See your doctor or visit a health clinic. You can help prevent more infections by always drinking plenty of water and also by drinking cranberry juice and eating plain yogurt that contains "live active cultures." If you are sexually active, doctors advise urinating immediately after intercourse.

Maintaining Healthy Genitals

You may have heard about *douching*.[3] This is generally not a good idea for a lot of reasons:

- Like washing your eyes, it's just not necessary.
- Your vagina produces natural fluids that help protect it from infections.

The thing you have to keep in mind is to gently wash the vaginal opening, the labia, and all of the folds.

Dry yourself thoroughly before putting on clean cotton underpants. Cotton underwear is best; synthetic fabric can cause irritation by trapping bacteria in the genital area. Cotton lets your body breathe.

Remember that it's very important to always wipe yourself with toilet paper from front to back. Urine or vaginal discharge will not harm the anus.

[3] douching (dooshing): using a container, tubing, and a nozzle to rinse the vagina.

9.

Having Your Period

Many girls feel that the most important change to occur during puberty is getting your period. A girl or woman menstruates, or has her period, about once a month as part of her *menstrual* cycle.

Starting *menstruation*[1] is a big deal because it means that you're now capable of becoming pregnant.

Some important things to remember about menstruation:
- All girls and women menstruate until they are in their mid- to late forties or early fifties.
- Menstruation won't hurt you or make you sick.
- Other people can't tell if you've gotten your period yet, or when you have it.

---

[1] menstruation (men-stroo-a-tion)

- While menstruating you can do anything that you would normally do, such as bathe, shampoo your hair, and exercise (even swim).

How Menstruation Happens

Most girls begin menstruating at around age eleven or twelve, but periods can start as early as nine or as late as seventeen. You can probably expect your first menstrual period about two years after you see breast buds, or a year or so after you've developed pubic hair.

I described the hormonal process that leads to menstruation in Chapter 5. But to recap: Once each month, your brain sends a hormone to your ovaries that causes the ova (eggs) inside to grow ripe. As this is happening, another hormone, *estrogen,* begins to build up inside the small sac that contains the ovum.

One of the ova will get larger than the others because it has more estrogen. When it is fully mature, it will burst out of its sac and be swept up into the *Fallopian tube,* through which it travels to your uterus, or womb. This is called *ovulation.*[2]

Meanwhile, another female sex hormone, *progesterone,* signals the *endometrial lining* of the uterus to build up a soft, thick cushion of blood vessels, tissue, and fluids. This serves as a nest to nourish and protect a fertilized egg to grow into a baby.

If the ovum is not fertilized, this cushion breaks down and flows through the cervix and out of the woman's vagina, to-

---

[2]   ovulation (ov-yuh-**ley**-shun)

gether with the blood-filled endometrial (uterine) lining, which is no longer needed. This process is what is called *menstruation,* or "having a period." When one month's menstruation is com-

pleted, the cycle begins all over again—the uterine lining begins to rebuild, the eggs (ova) begin to grow inside their little sacs, and eventually an egg is released. This is what is called the *menstrual cycle.*

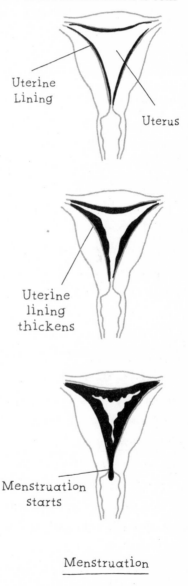

Uterine Lining

Uterus

Uterine lining thickens

Menstruation starts

Menstruation

Anticipating Your Period

If you have not yet gotten your period, now is the time to start thinking about what sanitary protection you will want.

Put a pad or tampon in your purse, your backpack, your locker, or in whatever other bag you carry with you, just in case. You can usually find these products in vending machines in women's bathrooms, or a school nurse will likely have some products on hand for emergencies.

If you can't get a sanitary product, fold up some toilet paper and put it in your underpants until you can get other protection.

If, during your period, blood leaks through your underpants onto your clothes, don't sweat it. Just wrap a sweater or sweatshirt around your waist or keep an extra pair of underpants, or even a skirt or pair of pants, inside your locker so you can change. To remove a bloodstain, use cold water to soak or rinse it out. Hot water will set the bloodstain into the fabric. If you're changing your tampons or pads frequently, this shouldn't happen as often.

The Menstrual Flow

Menstrual blood can be red, dark red, pink, or brown. You won't be able to see the egg, because it's much too tiny and has already started to dissolve. Throughout the day, your flow may vary from little dribbles to big gushes. You may feel the difference. There is no way to affect the amount of the flow.

Usually the flow is heavier for the first two days and then gets lighter and lighter. You may go an entire day without seeing any blood, and then see some the next day. Panty liners (discussed on p. 000) are a good solution.

Keeping Track of Your Menstrual Cycle

Menstrual periods occur anywhere from twenty-five to forty days apart. If your periods are regular, over time you can begin to anticipate when to expect your next period by keeping a calendar.

Put an *X* on the first day of your period and then on every day till your period ends. The next month, do the same, and, over time, you will be able to see a pattern of how many days you have be-
tween periods. The length of your cycle is from the first day of one period to the first day of the next, so if your period starts on a Tuesday and then starts on a Tuesday four weeks later, you have a twenty-eight-day cycle. You can download a menstrual calendar from the Internet to help you keep track of your periods. You will be

asked the first day of your last menstrual cycle each time you go to your doctor.

If you get cramps or premenstrual syndrome (PMS), you might also mark that on the calendar so you'll have a better sense of what to expect.

When you first begin menstruating, your periods will probably be irregular. You might even skip a month completely. Even if your schedule is regular, it can change if you lose or gain a lot of weight, get sick, travel, or exercise a lot.

Over time, though, most women's cycles become regular. If after six months or so, your periods haven't settled into a regular schedule of about once a month, check with your doctor.

Menstrual Protection

Most stalls in public women's bathrooms have a covered box hanging on the side, where you are asked to throw out pads, tampons, or panty liners so they won't clog the sewer pipes.

Pads

Sanitary pads (also called "napkins") fit inside the crotch of your underpants. They're held in place by a piece of adhesive tape that fastens them to the crotch fabric. Some pads have tape just on the back, and others have side wings that also wrap around the crotch to hold them more firmly. You pull off the strip of paper over the tape and press the pad into place. When the pad becomes almost saturated, just pull it off and dispose of it in a garbage.

Some girls like pads because they're simple to use and quick to change, and with them it is easy to see what's going on with your flow. They don't irritate your vagina and won't cause infection.

Pads come in all sizes, shapes, and widths. They also vary in thickness from "maxi pads," for heavier flows, to "mini pads," for lighter flows. Try different types to decide which does the best job for which day and feels the most comfortable.

Tampons

Some girls use both a pad and a tampon during the heaviest days of flow. By the way, using tampons doesn't make you a nonvirgin! A tampon fits inside the vagina, where it's held in place by the muscles. It has a string that hangs outside your

Panty Liner

Mini Pad

Slender or
Junior Pad

Regular
Maxi Pad

Super
Maxi Pad

Pad with
Wings

Kinds of Maxi Pads

body so that you can pull it out. If the string works its way into your vagina, you can use a finger to pull it back down, or you can always use your fingers to pull the tampon out.

Some teenage girls can use tampons as soon as they start

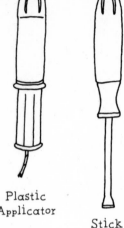

No
Applicator

Plastic
Applicator

Stick
Applicator

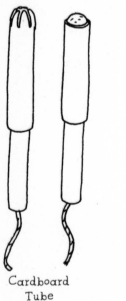

Cardboard
Tube
Applicators

Tampon
shape
after use

Kinds of Tampons

menstruating. They keep you dry, they don't show under any clothing, and they can be worn while swimming.

Like pads, tampons are made in different thicknesses for heavier and lighter flows, from "junior" to "super plus." They also come with different types of applicators:

- Cardboard applicator
- Plastic applicator
- Stick applicator
- No applicator—you push in the tampon with your finger.

It's best at first to use the slimmest tampons and those that are inserted with an applicator—many girls like the plastic ones that have rounded tips.

Try larger tampons, or the type that you push in with your finger, after you get used to them.

How to Insert a Tampon

When you first try a tampon, re-move the outer wrapper. Holding it in the middle with your thumb and middle finger, use your fore-fingers to practice pushing it back and forth through the applicator. Remove the sheet of paper from the box, read the instructions, and look at the diagram. Decide whether you want to try inserting the tampon while sitting on the toilet, standing with one foot on the toilet, or lying down. Most important, be sure to relax!

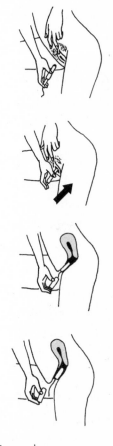

- Wash your hands thor-oughly.
- Never use a tampon with a torn wrapper.
- Make sure that the string hangs outside the bottom of the applicator.

Inserting a Tampon

- You might want to put a dab of lubricant, like K-Y jelly or Vaseline, on the tip of the tampon so that it will be easier to slide it into the vagina.
- Use your other hand to find your vaginal opening,

and spread it apart with your fingers. If you need to, look in a hand mirror.

- Take a deep breath, relax, and slide in the tip of the applicator, aiming it at a slight angle toward your back. This will not hurt.
- Guide the applicator into your vagina until your fingers touch your body, then use your forefinger to push on the inner tube until the tampon is all the way into your vagina.
- Pull out the applicator and throw it into the trash.
- Check that the tampon string hangs between your thighs.
- You should not feel the tampon in place. If you do, it's probably not inserted far enough in. You can either push it farther in with your finger or pull it out and start over with a new tampon.
- Wash your hands again when you're finished.
- To remove the tampon, just relax and pull it out with the string, and dispose of it in the garbage, not the toilet.

Don't feel bad if at first it's hard for you to insert a tampon. And don't worry if you poke yourself, because you won't do any damage. Just keep practicing. And by the way, the tampon can't get lost inside you!

If your flow is light, you'll want to change the tampon every three to four hours. On heavier days you may need to change a pad or tampon every couple of hours. If your flow is heavy enough that you need to change your pad or tampon every hour for several hours, or if you have to get up at night to change your pad or tampon, that is too heavy and you should see your family doctor.

If you just can't insert a tampon no matter how hard you try, see a doctor to find out what's going on.

Panty Liners

Panty liners, also sometimes called panty shields, are like pads except that they are so much thinner and lighter that you hardly know you're wearing one. They're good for those times when

- your flow is light.
- you're expecting your period to start.
- you wear a tampon and you're worried that it will leak. Tampons can leak a little even when they're inserted correctly.
- you're not sure that your period is over, and you want to feel safe for a day or two afterward.

Liners come in different sizes and shapes with a few types of absorbencies, but they don't vary as much as pads or tampons.

When to Use What

You don't have to choose among a pad, a tampon, or a liner. If your flow is very heavy, you can use both a tampon and a pad. If you know that your flow changes a lot from heavy to light, you might want to have a few different types of pads and tampons so you can switch back and forth.

How Often Must You Change Your Protection?

How often you need to change your protection depends, of course, on how heavy your flow is. But to stay healthy and avoid the chance of leaks, it's best to open a new pad, tampon, or liner every three or four hours. Wrap up the used pad, tampon, applicator, or liner in toilet paper, and throw it in the garbage. Never flush it down the toilet, because even brands that claim to be flushable can clog the pipes.

Do You Need a Deodorant During Menstruation?

Pads, tampons, and liners all come in both scented (deodorant) and unscented versions. The chemicals in scented products can irritate skin and cause allergic reactions, but if you don't get those symptoms, you can use them. However, you don't need them! As long as you wash and dry yourself thoroughly each day, wear clean underpants, and change your pads or tampons often, you won't have menstrual odor. When you urinate while wearing a tampon, hold the string out of the way so that it doesn't get wet, and if it does anyway, squeeze it dry with a tissue.

Problems That Can Arise

If menstrual problems are severe enough to interfere with your usual life, see a doctor. Some problems are:

- *Dysmenorrhea*[3]—when you have really strong cramps
- *Menorrhagia*[4]—when you have very heavy bleeding, periods that last longer than seven days, a cycle that is less than twenty-one days, or bleeding with clots
- *Amenorrhea*[5]—when you stop getting your periods after they have become fairly regular, or it has been two years since you've first started your breast development and still do not have a period. If you are already menstruating amenorrhea can result from stress, weight loss, thyroid disorder, or other medical conditions.
- Premenstrual Syndrome (PMS): when you experience symptoms, in the days leading up to your next period, including mood swings or irritability, tension or anxiety, anger or sadness, food cravings, breast tenderness. A good number of women will experience some of these symptoms. If your symptoms of PMS are severe, see your doctor. There are a variety of treatments for PMS.

Toxic Shock Syndrome

One thing you should never do is leave a tampon in place for more than six hours. It could cause a rare but serious infection

---

[3] dysmenorrhea (dis-men-uh-**ree**-uh)
[4] menorrhagia (men-uh-**rey**-jee-uh)
[5] amenorrhea (ey-men-uh-**ree**-uh)

called toxic shock syndrome. Anybody can get toxic shock, with or without wearing a tampon, but it occurs most often in girls and women who use them. Symptoms include a sudden high fever, low blood pressure, vomiting or diarrhea, a rash, muscle aches, seisures, and headaches.

Toxic shock is very rare, and you can avoid it easily if you follow these tips:

- Always wash your hands before inserting a tampon or putting your finger into your vagina.
- Keep your fingernails trimmed short and filed smooth.
- Use tampons during the day and use a pad at night.
- Don't use "superabsorbent" tampons. Use "slender" or "regular" ones unless you have very heavy flow.
- Change your tampons at least every six hours.
- Switch to pads when your flow lightens.

Fertilization and Pregnancy

If a sperm that has traveled up into the uterus fertilizes the mature egg, and the egg attaches itself to the uterine wall, the menstrual cycle stops because you are pregnant.

If you stop menstruating and you have had sexual intercourse, you should take a pregnancy test as soon as possible. Even if you have never had a period, if you have had penile-vaginal intercourse you could get pregnant anyway. An egg may have been released and you don't know it yet. This is one reason why you must not engage in unprotected sexual intercourse even if you haven't yet menstruated.

For more information on protection, see Chapter 13.

Perimenopause

All through adulthood, your hormones will continue to regulate your periods until you reach your forties. At this time the levels of your sex hormones will begin to drop and your periods may become irregular. This stage is called *perimenopause*.[6]

Menopause

Roughly about the time you're in your early fifties, your periods will stop for good. This is because the level of estrogen in older women drops and they no longer make mature eggs. This time in life is called *menopause*.[7]

---

[6] perimenopause (peri-**men**-uh-pawz)
[7] menopause (**men**-uh-pawz)

III

Sexuality

10.

Sexuality, Abstinence, and Sexual Intercourse

Sexuality

By nature, we are all sexual beings, from the time we are born to the time we die. This is one of the most beautiful parts of being human. During adolescence, you are learning to bring all aspects of yourself into relationship—your values, thoughts, emotions, and, yes, your sexuality. This is part of your identity. Understanding and becoming comfortable with your sexuality is an ongoing, lifelong process, as important as developing your mind and character. As you mature, this is what lets you join with another person to give and receive pleasure as well as to have babies.

Sexuality isn't just about having sex, as in sexual intercourse.

Sexuality is also about thoughts, fantasies, feelings—thinking sexy thoughts, feeling turned on, when we feel excited to see a person who appeals to us. It's those sexy feelings that make us want to kiss and hug and dance close.

Sexuality in its totality (kissing, fondling, and so forth), and sexual intercourse specifically, is too important, too potentially beautiful (and too potentially harmful—both physically and emotionally), to enter into without being thoughtful.

There are many joys, but also complications, that can arise when you have sexual intercourse. There are the risks of getting pregnant or getting someone pregnant or getting a sexually transmitted infection (STI) that could affect you for the rest of your life. Then there are the emotional risks of having your heart broken if you've given yourself to someone you don't really know, or trust, or aren't with for very long. While some high school relationships last a long time—maybe a lifetime—more often they are short-lived.

I am stunned by how many girls, when asked how they came to have their first intercourse, reply, "I don't know—it just happened"! You don't want your first time to "just happen," do you? Don't you want to be able to look back on it as an important, beautiful experience, not an uncomfortable, empty one? Your first time should be special. Of course, even if the first time is an uncomfortable one, over time and with maturity, your sexual experiences can become wonderful. Don't just give it away.

Abstinence

The very best, safest, smartest thing you can do is wait. Waiting is also called *abstinence*. To abstain means to wait—to hold off.

There are many very positive aspects to waiting: You won't have to worry about getting pregnant or getting your partner pregnant; you won't have to worry about getting an STI, including HIV; you won't have to worry about making a decision every time you go out with someone; you will feel good about living your values; you'll have something to look forward to; and you will learn to enjoy all the beautiful aspects of romance that don't involve sexual intercourse.

Why Waiting Can Make Sex Better

Actually, waiting until you are ready to have sex can make the experience better, and here is why. There should be a freedom from inhibition during sex with a trusted partner. Given that sexual arousal stems from a mind-body connection, you do not want unnecessary worries to interrupt your feelings of sexual pleasure. If you move ahead with sex without thinking things through, you might feel self-conscious about what you are doing. You could experience nagging thoughts about catching a disease, about whether you really like this person enough, about becoming pregnant or getting someone pregnant. It will disrupt your ability to stay aroused or have an orgasm.[1] If nothing else, it certainly will put a damper on the

---

[1] orgasm (**awr**-gaz-uhm): a strong surge of sexual pleasure, marked by rhythmic muscle contractions around the genitals in women and ejaculation in men

satisfaction you could have if you waited to have sex at the right time, in the right type of relationship.

Taking an Abstinence Pledge

If you are a member of a religious congregation, you may have been taught the value of abstinence. Some religious groups ask their young congregants to take an "abstinence pledge" to remain virgins until they are married.

It is important to pay attention to the values you have been brought up with. Beginning at this stage of your life, it is good to give a lot of thought to those values and what they mean—especially what they mean for you. To stick to those values, you need to make them your own, not just go along because some adult told you to.

Knowledge Is Power

Even if you have never had sex, even if you have taken an abstinence pledge, it is important to be fully informed about how to prevent pregnancy and sexually transmitted infections. These are just normal parts of life that you need to know about, and now is the time to learn, if you haven't already. There is a wise saying, "Knowledge is power." The more you understand about something, the more power you have to handle it when the time comes.

Becoming Turned On

What exactly is going on when you become turned on? Enjoying any type of sexual experience, from kissing to having intercourse, involves changes in your level of physical arousal. The first stage is really mental. They say the brain is the largest sex organ. It relates to your overall mood, your level of attraction to a person, and your feelings about starting sexual activity with that person.

If you are really turned on, your brain sends messages to your organs. Your blood pressure changes, your heartbeat may go up, and there is increased blood flow to your genitals. Even your skin feels more sensitive. Boys achieve erections and girls experience vaginal lubrication and expansion of the vaginal canal. (See Chapters 4 and 5 for explanations of your body's reproductive parts.) Girls will also find that their clitoris becomes larger and their nipples may become erect. People usually maintain this state of pleasurable arousal for some time until either they reach a *climax* (an orgasm) or they discontinue their sexual activity. As I said before, if you do not feel aroused, stop what you are doing. The time or the person is not right for you.

Fantasizing

Some people like to think sexy thoughts about someone who attracts them or about doing sexy things while they make love or masturbate. This is called *fantasizing.* There is nothing wrong with fantasizing. It is a good way to learn what turns you on.

Masturbation

Masturbation is a natural and safe way to express sexuality throughout our lives. Many people discover masturbation when they are young (even babies). Don't for one minute think that you are weird or the only person to do it. And, boys, you should know that girls masturbate, too, and so do grandmothers and grandfathers. People, after all, remain sexual well into old age.

Masturbation and Boys

If you are a boy, masturbating means stroking or rubbing your penis, "bed or pillow humping," or even just fantasizing to the point where you experience sexual pleasure. When masturbation lasts long enough and if you are old enough to be making sperm, it can result in ejaculation (usually beginning between ages eleven and sixteen). In fact, most boys first experience ejaculation while masturbating. It is a safe way to privately and safely release the buildup of sexual tension and to learn about what pleases you, what your body enjoys. And don't worry—you won't run out of sperm by masturbating, it won't affect your athletic performance, and it is not something you will have to stop when you are older and begin to have sex with someone. Similarly, it is not dangerous to become aroused, have an erection, and not ejaculate. The penis will simply relax into its softened state.

Masturbation and Girls

Girls masturbate for the same reason boys do. It is a safe and pleasurable way to release sexual tension. Girls masturbate by rubbing their clitoris and the area around and just inside their vaginas. They can do this with their hands or with a vibrator (a handheld device that vibrates) or by rubbing up against something that is hard. They do not ejaculate sperm like men do but they do have orgasms and a few women release fluid when they orgasm. This fluid is different from urine.

Not Everyone Masturbates

However, not all people masturbate and your family may not approve, so you need to be sensitive to their feelings. But you (and they) need to know that there is absolutely no medical evidence that masturbation can cause mental or physical damage!

When Is It Too Much?

Masturbation is just like anything else. If it's all you can think about, or if you can't stop doing it over and over many times a day, or if you do it so often that it interferes with school, chores, sports, family, or friends, then it's just as much a problem as anything else you might overdo. If this happens, or if masturbation makes you feel bad about yourself or guilty, then maybe you should stop and take time to think about why you have these feelings. Are they really yours, or are they feelings that others have imposed on you? Perhaps you should discuss your feelings with a parent, school counselor, clergyperson, or doctor.

Outercourse and Hooking Up

Some young people feel that "hooking up" or "messing around" is a casual thing to do. Kissing or touching someone's body without having intercourse can be called *outercourse.* I like this word better than the one your parents probably use, *foreplay,* because foreplay implies it is leading up to something more, such as *inter*course.

*Outer*course implies doing things that are pleasurable in and of themselves without penetration of any kind. Naturally, deciding if or when to move ahead further with outercourse, from kissing to French kissing (using your tongue) or from kissing to petting (stroking breasts), for example, is different from having sexual intercourse. For instance, touching someone's breasts or genitals with your hands won't result in pregnancy. Nonetheless, heavy kissing and touching still involves powerful feelings, and in certain situations (hand or mouth to genitals), can involve transmission of sexually transmitted diseases.

Oral Sex

Let's define what is meant by *oral sex.* The medical definition of *sex* is any genital contact at all, whether hand to genitals, mouth to genitals, or genitals to genitals. Oral sex is the act of putting one's mouth, lips, or tongue on another person's genitals with the intention of sexually arousing and stimulating the other person to orgasm. *Cunnilingus*[2] is the term for orally

---

[2] cunnilingus (kuhn-l-**ing**-guhs)

stimulating a woman's vulva and clitoris. *Fellatio*[3] is the act of orally stimulating a man's penis. Performing oral sex on a boy is also called "giving head," "giving a blow job" or "going down on." When girls are receiving it is also called "going down on." Oral sex counts as sex.

Some people believe that oral sex is a way to remain a virgin and not have to worry about getting pregnant. Another belief is that it's a way to avoid getting an STI. This is not true.

You can get HIV, herpes, chlamydia, gonorrhea, and trichomoniasis through oral sex. You can also feel just as emotionally involved and therefore vulnerable. To avoid contracting an STI, you must perform fellatio with a condom and cunnilingus with a "dental dam" (a piece of latex covering the female's vulva).

Don't believe that oral sex doesn't count as sex. It does. I have talked with so many girls who have given their dates oral sex thinking that way they could keep their virginity. But afterward, they felt bad—about the experience and about themselves. Girls your age might do this as a way to keep a boyfriend or do what she thinks her friends are doing but, instead, it just gives her a reputation as being "easy" or "fast," gives pleasure to a boy who may not really care about her, and does nothing for her except, maybe, give her an STI that may never go away! Some boys try to talk girls into giving them oral sex by saying that sperm prevents breast cancer or that it "makes your skin glow." Girls, show you're smarter than they think and just laugh at these myths.

No matter what anyone says, oral sex is an intimate act for

---

[3] fellatio (fuh-**lay**-shee-oh)

both partners that can leave you feeling used and ashamed if you are not with someone you care about and who cares about you. It can, however, be a beautiful and satisfying experience if you are old enough, in a loving, sensual, trusting relationship.

Orgasm

During orgasm, you will experience a strong surge of sexual pleasure, marked by rhythmic muscle contractions around your genitals. Some orgasms can be short in duration and give you sensations right around your genitals, while other orgasms may last longer and feel like a powerful, full-body experience. After orgasm, your body goes through a resolution phase that is often marked by a sense of relaxation, tension reduction, and well-being.

11.

The Decision to Have Sex, Communication About Sex, and Common Questions

The Decision to Have Sex

The decision about when to begin to have sexual intercourse is affected by how you were raised, your religious beliefs and values, your age, what your parents have told you about how they feel on the subject (if they've discussed these things at all), and when you are in a loving relationship. The goal is to wait until you have a committed relationship with a trusting partner with whom you can freely communicate.

Ultimately, the decision to become sexually active is your own. This gives you a lot of freedom but it also requires thoughtfulness and responsibility.

What is most critical is that your decision about moving to a more serious, sexual relationship is just that, serious, as opposed to it just happening in the heat of passion, or because you were drinking, or were pressured, or wanted to "get it over with" or to "see what all the fuss is about."

How Far Do High School Kids Go with Sexuality?

Some friends may tell you that they've done all sorts of sexual things, and this may make you feel bad if you haven't. But, in fact, over the past years, fewer girls and guys are engaging in more advanced sexual acts. And you should not feel there's anything wrong with you if you do not date or kiss, have sex, or have any high school romances.

No Matter What You Decide, Communication Is Key

Perhaps the best way to tell if you are in a real relationship as opposed to an infatuation is if you can communicate openly and freely. Communication is the key to healthy sexual decision-making. Whether you want to delay sex, start sex, or have more satisfying sex, you need to be able to *talk* about sex. In an intimate relationship you should be able to have open discussions about all sorts of things—even topics that might make you blush or feel insecure. Good decisions about sexual activity require honest conversations with your sexual partner.

Communicating About Sex Is Hard

Don't be discouraged if you find it hard to talk about sex—so do lots of adults. You may have been raised to keep your sexual organs covered and to be quiet about any topic that was related to your genitals or sexual feelings. Ironically, now that you are a teenager, you need to relearn how to talk about these intimate, once "forbidden" topics.

It is also very important to have open communication with your partner before you start having sex because part of being in a responsible, mature relationship involves getting tested for STIs if either of the partners in the relationship has been sexually active in the past. Before you start having sex with someone, it is important to know that neither partner has an STI. You need to be able to feel comfortable asking if your partner has ever had sex before and asking him or her to get tested. Someone giving you his or her word about not having an STI is not enough. STIs will be discussed more in Chapter 14. But having this conversation about getting tested is an important part of communicating with your boyfriend or girlfriend.

You Need to Know and Trust Your Intimate Partner

You can't trust your partner if you can't communicate honestly. Ideally, any amount of physical intimacy should be matched with an equal amount of emotional intimacy. When you know and trust someone, you are much more likely to have safe and satisfying sexual experiences with him or her. If you do not know someone well, any type of sexual interaction could be risky—both physically and emotionally.

Setting Boundaries

If you feel you are in a healthy relationship, it is always a good idea to make your boundaries clear before getting too far into it. This isn't something to do right away, but as the relationship develops you will need to say what you expect. Here are some examples of things that might be important to you: being faithful, being truthful, not gossiping about each other, not doing anything sexual that the two of you have not already agreed to. It's sort of like a personal contract.

Here are some ways to open the lines of communication and set boundaries:

- "I want to know how far you want this to go."
- "I need to tell you something."
- "Wait, I am confused about what you want."
- "I want to keep kissing you but I don't want to have sex."
- "What we are trying isn't quite right for me, can we try _____?"

Take notice of your own body language. Try to be clear with your partner and keep your verbal messages in line with your body language. Do not, for instance, smile and say, "Maybe later," if you really mean "No." Remember that no one is a mind reader—if you send an unclear message, you will not be understood.

Telling the Truth

If you feel you are in a good, loving relationship and want to get more serious, it is fine to just say to your partner, "I need to know if you're having sex with someone else." This is a normal, smart, healthy thing to want to know, and so just ask. If you later find out the person was lying to you, you know this isn't a relationship you want to stay in.

Do you trust that you can tell the truth about your feelings to your partner and not have it used against you? Do you feel that he or she makes an effort to really hear and understand you? A healthy relationship is one where you can tell the other person if he or she has hurt you or if you're feeling distance between you. Then the two of you can talk it through.

This does not mean that you necessarily should be talking about all of this yet. There is nothing immature about holding off on these conversations if they don't apply to you right now. For some of you, your conversations may relate to how you like to be kissed . . . and it's good to be able to talk about kissing if your partner doesn't quite understand the way you like it. Pleasure matters, and sometimes it takes talking and practice to arrive at mutual pleasure.

Look Beneath the Surface

Not that this is the time in your life when you're looking for a lifelong partner, but it may be a good time to learn to look beneath the surface of someone you are considering hooking up with. Is he or she kind? Considerate? Capable of respecting you? Is he or she all about bravado and show or is there substance beneath what may be a flashy exterior?

When Is It Not a Healthy Relationship?

It is not a healthy relationship if there is abuse or pressure of any kind. You should not allow disrespectful language, subtle pressure, or deception in an intimate relationship. It should go without saying that anyone who puts you down, uses violence against you, or tries to force you into sex is an unhealthy partner. You should never tolerate any form of physical, verbal, emotional, or sexual abuse in what is supposed to be a loving relationship. It is also wrong for your partner to threaten to hurt him- or herself as a way to pressure you to do things you may not want to do. Even if your partner eventually apologizes for this behavior, it is still destructive and should not be tolerated. Be wary of partners who are obsessively jealous and paranoid, always suspicious and accusing, even if all you're doing is talking to someone else. Boyfriends or girlfriends who call you constantly, check your cell phone or Facebook page, want to know where you are and who you are with, are stepping over the line. While you may be flattered at first, this is an unhealthy relationship.

Don't stay in an abusive relationship thinking you can change your partner! It never works. See the end of this chapter for information about healthy dating attitudes and relationships as well as resources for what to do if you are in an unhealthy relationship.

It goes without saying that if your partner lies to you or uses your relationship to make him- or herself look good, it is not a healthy relationship.

Listen to Your Body

Another way to tell if you are in a healthy relationship is to listen to your body. Are your muscles tense? Is your breathing shallow? These are signs that you don't feel 100 percent safe. To be able to read your body's signals, you have to stay connected to your body. It is impossible to do this if you have had too much to drink or are spaced out on drugs.

Sexual Abuse

Some teenagers have been victims of sexual abuse as younger children. When they are in a relationship, it can feel very unsettling when sexual touching progresses. It can be very hard for someone who has been abused to say that he or she wants to stop. If you have been sexually abused, it makes sense that outercourse and sex could bring up difficult memories for you. See Chapter 15 for more about sexual abuse.

Communicating When You're *Not* Ready: Saying "No" and Meaning It

It is important to be prepared for how to handle it if the person you're with tries to convince you to move ahead sexually when you feel uneasy about it. Anytime you feel unsure about sex, the answer is "no." Anytime you feel afraid, the answer is "no." Anytime you feel turned off, the answer is "no." "No" never has to be justified. "No" is enough. Period.

Sometimes you will get pressured to engage in sex in subtle ways. Someone might say, "If you love me you will have sex with me." This shows he or she does not respect you. Your re-

sponse should be: "Wrong! If you love me you won't ask me to do something I don't feel ready for!"

Someone could say to you, "We did it before, so what's the problem?" or "I thought we loved each other!" or, if it's a boy, "I promise I will pull out." In these moments you must be true to yourself. If you don't want to have intercourse you should be ready to say things such as:

- "I don't want to do this."
- "No. That's my final answer."
- "I don't feel right about this. We are going to stop."

When You *Are* Ready, Communicating What Feels Good

There are many ways to tell your partner what feels good to you. Some people have direct conversations about the sexual acts they prefer. This is a good way to communicate, but it is not always easy for people. Many couples rely on subtle signals like soft sounds or body language. Saying things like "I like that," "Yeah," or "Keep doing that" are effective ways to indicate what feels good for you. You may also get your point across by gently guiding someone's hand or saying, "Mmm."

Body language alone simply does not suffice as effective sexual communication. If you rely on body language, you are likely to be misread or to misread someone's feelings or intentions. For instance, someone who is opposed to sexual intercourse before marriage may still want to kiss you or engage in outercourse. This is why it is so important to talk about sex. If you can't discuss sex, you're probably not ready for it.

Be gently inquisitive with your partner. Don't laugh at or put down your partner when he or she tries to talk about sex.

Disembodiment/Disassociation in Girls

It is essential to a girl's well-being that she knows and can experience what she is feeling. Researchers of girls' psychology have written that one cannot "cut off one kind of desire without affecting another." A girl's ability to love herself and to know what she wants will be reduced if she has cut off her feelings of sexual desire, and "then becomes especially vulnerable to the power of others' feelings as well as to what others say she does and does not want or feel." (Deborah L. Tolman, *Dilemmas of Desire: Teenage Girls Talk About Sexuality,* Cambridge, MA; Harvard University Press, 2002, p. 21.)

If a girl is clear about her body's feelings, she will know when things between her and her partner are heating up too much and will know when to stop. She will be more able to talk about how she is feeling with her partner in a way that includes how she feels and that makes it possible to discuss then how both people feel. Sex won't "just happen."

How Do You Know the Correct Technique?

You might feel confused about how to please a sexual partner. When you are new at something, you naturally wonder if you are doing things right. But remember, there is no sexual technique that pleases everyone the same way. What turns you on has a lot to do with feelings, intentions, and fantasies. All of these relate to what is going on in your brain. So don't worry too much about exactly where or how to touch someone. Don't think about sex as though it is an achievement test you'll be graded on. Pleasurable sex is impossible if you're burdened with performance anxiety. There is no mechanical function, no button to push, that guarantees sexual arousal. Rather, satisfying sexual experiences are about feeling turned on, relaxed, present in your body, and safe in the relationship.

Pay Attention

Never move so fast during outercourse that you don't notice if it is mutually pleasurable. You can say something like, "Is this okay?" when you aren't sure about what your partner feels. Do not assume that because someone is quiet that he or she is comfortable with your actions. Some people become too intimidated to say that they want you to stop. Some people freeze up and stop communicating when they feel anxious or uncomfortable.

It is not always easy to tell if a girl is turned on. If she is tense, scared, or not turned on by her partner, intercourse can hurt. Only when a girl is aroused does her vagina relax and lubricate naturally. If you are not ready—either because you don't want to be doing it or because your partner has not been generous and taken sufficient time with outercourse—you should say so and stop.

Don't Fake It

Think about what having emotionally safe sex means. Some people work so hard at acting sexy or pleasing their partner, they do not give enough attention to their own true feelings or vulnerabilities. If you are putting on an act or "going through the motions" when you are engaged in a sexual activity, you are undermining your relationship and your self-esteem. Try to notice what your body is telling you at such times. As I have just said, there are often physical signs that reveal emotional truths such as discomfort or happiness. Notice whether you feel tension in your muscles or whether you feel relaxed. Observe whether your breathing is shallow or deep. Be aware if there are any little thoughts you are trying to push out of your mind. These internal clues may help you recognize if you truly are comfortable with what you are doing or who you are with. And if you are not truly turned on, stop what you are doing. Maybe you are with the wrong person. Maybe the person you're with doesn't care enough to pay attention to how you are feeling.

Waiting until you establish emotional intimacy is not prudish or old-fashioned; it just makes good sense. You can avoid having unprotected or unsatisfying sex by giving yourself time.

Common Questions and Issues

She Only Wants to Be Friends!
In talking with high school boys, I sometimes hear this: "I treat my girlfriend very nicely. I respect her and don't force myself on her, but she only sees me as a friend, not someone to go with. She prefers dating the players. What can I do?"

I am very touched by these boys and, to better know how to respond to them, I asked Paul Kivel, who has written many books for and about boys, how he would respond. Paul said, "If they are heterosexual, there are a lot of different kinds of girls out there with many different interests and desires. Just like it takes a while to sort out who your close friends are, it can take a while to sort out who you match with as a boyfriend/girlfriend."

Paul pointed out that many men these boys know (fathers, uncles, brothers, neighbors, coaches, and so forth) probably don't fit the "player" stereotype and yet they have found loving partners. In fact, most men don't actually fit the player model and end up in healthy, loving relationships.

"Relationships cannot last and be close and loving unless both people can be themselves and express their feelings to each other," Paul said. So, to those boys who feel bad because girls don't view them as "players," I say, "Be patient. Be who you are and you are likely to find, sooner or later, the right love for you . . . one with integrity, respect, and intimacy."

All of this is true for girls as well.

Girls: What If You Don't Have an Orgasm?

Not everyone has an orgasm every time she engages in vaginal intercourse. This can be because she doesn't feel safe or comfortable with her partner or she doesn't feel confident enough to be relaxed. Perhaps she hasn't been sufficiently aroused during outercourse.

Many women are unable to have an orgasm with vaginal intercourse alone and require stimulation of the clitoris, the most sensitive part of a woman's vaginal area, in order to orgasm. In some women, the clitoris isn't close enough to the opening of the vagina to be stimulated by the penis during intercourse.

If a man has not had an orgasm but his partner has and wants to stop, the man can masturbate himself (or ask his partner to masturbate him) until he reaches orgasm. (Or he can simply allow his erection to subside.) A woman could do the same.

Boys: What If You Can't Get an Erection?

There are many reasons that a man doesn't get an erection when he is expected to. It may be the wrong time, the wrong partner, he may be nervous because this really matters to him, he may have had too much to drink or be on drugs, or he may be taking a medication that prevents his getting an erection.

Many fine lovers fail to get an erection sometimes. It may also mean that the person a man is with is so important to him that he freezes up. Or it can mean you are not the right partners for each other.

Pregnancy

A female can become pregnant anytime a couple has vaginal intercourse unless she's already pregnant. No matter how regular her menstrual cycle seems to be, a female can never know for sure that neither of her ovaries has released an egg. An ovum can live twelve to twenty-four hours after ovulation, and sperm can live in the vagina or uterus for three to five days. Sperm in the vagina before you have intercourse can fertilize an egg that comes into the uterus after intercourse, so there is a period of several days during each cycle when you can become pregnant. That's a lot of time in which the sperm and egg can meet. Sperm don't even have to start within the vagina—if any semen lands on a female's vulva, sperm can swim into the vagina through her lubricant.

In Chapter 13 we'll look at all the ways you and your partner can avoid pregnancy if you are sexually active and, if pregnancy does occur, what decisions the two of you might make. We'll be talking about safer sex and avoiding sexually transmitted infections (STIs) in Chapter 14.

Resources

- Go Ask Alice!: This website, run by Columbia University, is a great resource for teens to ask questions online and get honest answers about sex, relationships, and health in general. You can write in your own question and you can read others' questions.
  www.goaskalice.columbia.edu

- Love Is Respect: This organization is dedicated to engaging, educating, and empowering youth and young adults to prevent and end abusive relationships. In addition to the helpful information on their website, they have the National Dating Abuse Helpline, which teens can access 24/7 through online chat, text, or phone. Text LOVE IS to 77054 or call 1–866–331–9474.
  www.loveisrespect.org
  www.loveisrespect.org/about-national-dating-abuse -helpline

- Break the Cycle: Empowering Youth to End Domestic Violence:
  www.breakthecycle.org

- Love Is Not Abuse:
  www.loveisnotabuse.com

12.

Sexual Orientation and Gender Identity

Sexual Orientation

Sexual orientation describes who a person is sexually attracted to. Sexual orientation is just one part of who a person is.

People who are sexually attracted to people of the other sex are called *heterosexual* or "straight." People who are sexually attracted to someone of the same sex are called *homosexual* or "gay." Women who are sexually attracted to other women also refer to themselves as *lesbians*. Some people are *bisexual* or "bi," meaning that they are sexually attracted to people of both sexes. People who are simply not "straight" but do not fit into any of these categories exclusively may also refer to themselves as "queer." People who are still trying to figure out their sexual identity sometimes refer to themselves as *questioning*.

Thus the acronym LGBTQ stands for "lesbian, gay, bisexual, transgender, or questioning" and includes all people who do not identify as straight or heterosexual.

Gender Identity

Heterosexual people are born feeling comfortable being the gender they appear to be and they are attracted to people of the opposite sex. They can flirt and date openly without being harassed; they can have children together; it is they who are most commonly represented in the mainstream media.

Some people feel that they've been born with an incorrectly assigned gender. A biological man feels more like a woman or vice versa. These people are *transgender* or "trans."

Sexual orientation describes who you are attracted to, whereas *gender identity* describes who you feel you are. One describes a sexual impulse toward something external, and the other is an internal identity. As a trans friend of mine puts it, "Gender identity is who you want to see in your mirror. Sexuality is who you want to hold hands with on the Ferris wheel." I will write more about trans youth later in this chapter.

Not Being Heterosexual Is Not a Matter of Choice

Being gay, lesbian, or bisexual is sometimes referred to as a lifestyle or a choice. This is not true. We don't choose our sexual orientation or our sexual identity.

Scientists today believe that sexual orientation is a natural trait, just like a person's body type or hair color. According to the American Psychological Association (APA), "Most scientists today agree that sexual orientation is most likely the result of a complex interaction of environmental, cognitive, and biological factors. . . . There is also considerable . . . evidence to suggest that biology, including genetic or inborn hormonal factors, play[s] a significant role."

The APA also says, "Homosexuality is not an illness. It does not require treatment and is not changeable." In fact, the association states that therapy to try to make gay people straight or make trans people change the way they feel can harm them psychologically. The most recent survey, conducted in 2012 by Gallup, suggests that 6.4 percent of people ages eighteen to twenty-nine identify as gay.

Not So Different from "Straight" People

On some level, it is odd to have a separate chapter on this subject because all the subjects in this book are relevant to gay, lesbian, bisexual, and transgender teenagers. No matter your sexual orientation or gender identity, you will feel similar excitement (and worries) when you become attracted to someone. You will wonder if the person likes you back. You could fret about the right time to reveal your feelings. You might find it awkward to move ahead with sexual behaviors or talk about safer sex. These are experiences just about everybody shares.

Gay, lesbian, bisexual, and transgender people are more like "straight" people than they are different. They can be any age, race, religion, or background, and may have any job you can imagine. They may fall in love with and share their entire lives with another person, just as straight people do.

They can have their own children or adopt and provide as stable and loving a family as a straight couple can. Some U.S. states recognize same-sex marriage, and many more allow gay people to adopt children. If gay partners choose not to adopt children, they can have biological children of their own. A lesbian couple can use donated sperm to become pregnant, or a female friend might agree to become pregnant with the sperm from a gay male couple.

Children raised in same-sex families are no different from those who live with both a female and a male parent, with one biological and one stepparent, with adoptive or foster parents, with separated or divorced parents, or with a single parent. They're no different from children raised by grandparents or other relatives or even family friends. Families come in all forms.

What's important is that the children are well loved and cared for. Having a baby requires enormous amounts of time, attention, and resources. Many gay and trans people are wonderful, loving parents who relish the opportunity to raise families.

Can Sexual Orientation Shift Over Time?

Like many other things about sex, homosexuality disturbs some people. This is why teens might worry about any attraction they may ever feel toward somebody of the same sex. The thought of being gay might really not fit with how you always imagined yourself and your life. You might wonder what your family would think, and if they would still love you, if you were gay.

Sometimes, while you're growing up, you might become interested in a person of the same sex for a while and may want to experiment sexually with that person. You may have romantic feelings toward a person of the same sex. Teens may have straight or gay sex dreams at different times. This is perfectly normal. Experimentation does not determine your sexual orientation. Only with time will a person determine his or her sexual orientation. This may even continue to change over the course of his or her life.

Attitudes Toward Homosexuality

Throughout history and in all cultures there have been homosexual people who have been admired and hated. The ancient Greeks admired homosexual relationships. Over the years we have acquired a broader understanding of the role of homosexuality in history.

This was not always well understood because people have been forced to keep same-sex relationships secret, fearing discrimination. The reason that gay people have been afraid to be themselves is that they have been insulted, threatened, attacked, abused, murdered, and denied common rights that "straight" people take for granted. In fact, doctors used to treat homosexuality as a mental illness. Homosexuality is also viewed by some religions as a sin. Some people hate or fear homosexuals because they are afraid of people who are different. For these reasons, some gay people still have to hide who they are at times.

It's thought that 2 to 4 percent of people worldwide are gay. That statistic is pretty close to the number of people throughout the world who have blue eyes. Imagine if everybody thought it was okay to hate, fear, and abuse people just because they were born with blue eyes.

Homophobia

Unfortunately, there are added burdens when you grow up as a gay, lesbian, bisexual, or transgender teen. The most important challenge is homophobia in the culture—hatred of lesbian, gay, bi, trans, and questioning (LGBTQ) people—and the range of harassment, abuse, teasing, and violence these youth experience. They are too often treated as different, and are isolated by family and peers. They may have difficulty finding adult support. If you are lesbian, bisexual, gay, trans, or questioning, you may feel confused about your identity. Most teens go through some stress and anxiety as they come to terms with their sexuality, in any case. If you are growing up gay or feel as if you have been born with the wrong gender, odds are a lot of your mental energy has been spent just trying to figure out what your sexual orientation or gender identity is and in responding to the reactions or the hostility of those around you.

Many, many people, including straight ones, are confused about their sexuality. A good trained counselor may help you sort out your feelings and support you if you need help. At the end of this chapter I list resources you might turn to.

People Who Are Homophobic

People who are cruel to gays, lesbians, bisexuals, or trans people are often those who are unsure about their own sexuality. It is unfortunate that people feel that by hating gay, lesbian, bisexual, or trans youth, it proves that they are not like them. Being hateful or judgmental toward anyone is not right.

Some of these "haters" excuse their behavior by citing the Bible, saying that it calls homosexuality a sin. Let's remember the compassion and love that great teachers and leaders such as Jesus, Gandhi, Buddha, and Dr. Martin Luther King, Jr., showed to those who were different and, instead of hating, taught that we must learn to embrace difference. That is the truly wise, kind, compassionate, and right thing to do.

The Need for Support

Many young people are curious about same-sex attraction and need to talk to other people who have been through the same experience. Today, there are many, many support groups, websites, hotlines, and community centers for LGBTQ teens. Whoever you are, you have the right to explore your true feelings.

Currently in the United States there are nearly five thousand schools with Gay-Straight Alliance clubs that are registered with the Gay, Lesbian & Straight Education Network (GLSEN; see the end of this chapter for their website). The network is a national organization whose mission is to make sure that all students, regardless of their sexual orientation or gender identity, are safe and respected.

Compassion and Kindness

Regardless of a person's sexual orientation or gender identity, he or she deserves respect. It is hurtful and disrespectful to use words like "fag," "homo," or "dyke." While it is true that in some gay and lesbian communities the members may refer to themselves as "dyke" or "queer" as a term of endearment, no one should use these words disrespectfully. No one likes being called names.

If you are straight, think about how you would feel if you were called names because of your race or size. Always try to put yourself in the other person's shoes. Bullying is always wrong—all forms of it. Don't ever do it, or tolerate it. No matter what! If you see bullying happening, try to stop it. No one should be picked on for any reason, including sexual orientation or gender identity. Express your support and show your LGBTQ friends that you will not abandon them.

A gay or lesbian friend may need your help finding a supportive adult to talk to. Furthermore, if you have a friend who comes out to you, you should try to:

- listen quietly and attentively.
- tell him or her that what he or she is saying is important and you want him or her to feel comfortable talking with you.
- reassure him or her that you still care about him or her just as much as you did before.
- try to avoid downplaying or minimizing what he or she is saying to you.
- avoid laughing, seeming shocked, or saying you don't believe it.

Coming Out

Gay men, lesbians, trans, and bisexual people sometimes struggle with accepting their sexual orientation and telling other people—that is, coming out.

Keeping a secret about yourself can be exhausting. It is deeply stressful to feel that you are always putting on an act. In fact, it is very difficult to feel close to the people you love if you aren't honest with them. Still, coming out is a very personal process. Telling your friends and family about your sexual orientation can be scary but it could ultimately feel like a big relief. According to many advocates for gay, lesbian, bisexual, and trans teenagers, coming out can be one of the most important steps in creating a comfortable life for yourself.

Of course, not everyone is lucky enough to have an open-minded and accepting family. Furthermore, you may not live in a community that is tolerant of homosexuality. If this is your situation, it is best to have your initial conversations with the people you anticipate will be most accepting. This could be your parents, a good friend, a trusted aunt, uncle, or counselor. Some teenagers have to make a decision to be "out" among family members, but not at school, or vice versa. Most important, consider your health and safety first and try not to put yourself in danger.

Coming out to your family can be intimidating. It is ideal if you can talk directly with your parents, but you may be nervous about that. Some parents are particularly accepting and loving in these conversations. Your parents may even surprise you and tell you how proud they are of you for being honest and brave. This is the type of response you deserve.

It is possible, however, that your parents may feel confused and need some time to get used to the news. Some parents wonder if they did something that made you turn out gay, or initially feel disoriented because they always imagined you growing up a particular way. Some parents appear disappointed because they fear you won't get married or have children. There are parents who are so angry that they become abusive. If you want to be honest with your parents, but don't know how to talk to them, you may want to contact one of the support groups listed in the resources list at the end of this chapter.

Transgender Youth

Chaz Bono is the son of the iconic singers Sonny and Cher. Chaz was born a girl named Chastity. This is what he has to say about his transition from girl to boy: "I don't think the way I grew up had any effect on this issue. There is a gender in your brain and a gender in your body. For 99 percent of people, those things are in alignment. For transgender people, they are mismatched. That's all it is. It's not complicated, it's not a neurosis. It is a mix-up." (Cintra Wilson, "The Reluctant Transgender Role Model," *The New York Times,* May 8, 2011.)

The disconnect between the body they were born with and how they feel about their gender identity can be excruciatingly painful for transgender teens. Many children know at an early age—three or four years—that they are not the sex they appear to be, and they struggle when their parents force them to dress and behave like their birth gender. Many parents have no clue that their child is trans and are at a loss for what to do.

If you feel you are trans and think it is safe to discuss this with your parents, help yourself and them to understand all you can about what this means and how best to manage it by getting assistance from counselors and resources in the trans community. (See list of resources at the end of this chapter.)

Some parents decide to let their trans child behave, dress, and name themselves as their desired gender identity at home but not at school, at least not right away. Some decide to move their family to a new school where their trans child can start over as the gender they identify with and thus have less risk of being teased or bullied.

A growing number of teenagers who realize that, for whatever reason, they were misassigned at birth and want to realign who they are with how they think of themselves, decide to undertake medical, social, and legal steps to transition from their assigned (birth) gender to their true gender. This means going through the therapy, hormone treatments, and operations that will realign their "brain gender" and their "body gender." This is a brave thing to do. If you want to know more about transitioning, there are many places you can go for information and help. (See Resources at the end of this chapter.)

A Final Word to Gay, Lesbian, Bi, and Trans Youth

If you feel so lonely or misunderstood that you don't think life is worth living, please remember that situations change with time. Do not do anything dangerous and do not resort to hurting yourself. Try to remember that it gets easier to carve out a comfortable life as you understand yourself more

fully. There is a vast, welcoming community out there waiting for you. You will eventually be able to live wherever you
want and surround yourself with supportive and likeminded
friends.

Resources

Here are some places to go for information and support:
- The Hetrick-Martin Institute is a New York City–
  based nonprofit organization devoted to serving
  the needs of lesbian, gay, bisexual, transgender, or
  questioning (LGBTQ) youth. 1–212–674–2400.
- Indiana Youth Group. 1–800–347–TEEN.
- The Gay, Lesbian & Straight Education Network,
  GLSEN, an organization that works to end discrimination, harassment, and bullying based on
  sexual orientation, gender identity, and gender expression in K–12 schools.
  www.glsen.org
- PFLAG: Parents, Families and Friends of Lesbians
  and Gays
  www.pflag.org
- The Trevor Project: preventing suicide among
  LGBTQ youth.
  www.thetrevorproject.org
- The Point Foundation: LGBT scholarships.
  www.pointfoundation.org
- TYFA: TransYouth Family Allies
  www.imatyfa.org

- Lambda Legal: LGBT legal resources.
  www.lambdalegal.org
- Advocates for Youth is a nonprofit organization
  and advocacy group based in Washington, D.C.,
  dedicated to sexuality education, the prevention of
  HIV and of sexually transmitted disease, teenage
  pregnancy prevention, youth access to condoms
  and contraception, and equality for LGBT youth.
  www.advocatesforyouth.org
- mPowerment Project: HIV-prevention program
  designed to address the needs of young gay and
  bisexual men
  www.mpowerment.org

13.

Contraception, Pregnancy, and Options if You Become Pregnant

For seventeen years, through my nonprofit organization in Georgia, the Georgia Campaign for Adolescent Power & Potential, I have witnessed what happens when a girl gets pregnant and young people become parents before they have grown up themselves. The consequences are sobering.

Why You Must Plan for It

Pregnancy (and STIs) can happen to anyone who chooses to be sexually active—anyone, from any family, from any neighborhood, with any grades. That is why it is so important to think about contraception and STD protection before having sex. Beyond thinking about it, you need to plan for it. Every single time. Your first time, your next time, every time.

Consequences of Teen Pregnancy

Some girls have said they want to get pregnant because they're lonely and want someone to love them, or they think it will keep their boyfriend from leaving them. These are wrong assumptions. It is hard for teenage parents to have a stable relationship and to stay together. In most cases, teenage fathers are not able to provide adequate support for their teenage partner and their baby, even when they have a strong desire to do so. Roughly 75 percent of babies born to teenage parents will require some form of public assistance. Psychologists tell me that among adolescent married couples, relationship quality oftentimes goes downhill after a child is born because there is so much focus placed on caretaking, managing a household, and problem solving. Couples raising children generally do not describe their relationship as "an infatuated love affair" or even as "best friends." Rather, couples with young children will often describe their relationship more as "a practical partnership." Caring for a baby involves so much responsibility and attention to family matters there is much less time for fun or spontaneity. If you haven't already, check out the MTV series called *16 and Pregnant* and the follow-up series, *Teen Mom*. They give a realistic picture of how hard it is to be both pregnant and a teen mom.

It may seem as if it is the girl who bears the consequences of pregnancy and birth, and sometimes it is. She carries the child inside her, she gives birth, and much of the time she is the one who ends up caring for the baby. The culture makes some young men believe that a sign of manhood is having fathered many children with different women. Any mature, smart man knows, however, that true manhood means being responsible for one's actions and, for a young father, that means showing up as a co-parent.

Impact on the Child

Whatever the man's circumstances, he should be a presence in his child's life. It is as important for daughters to have loving, present fathers as it is for sons. Some mothers grew up without the presence of a father. Perhaps their own mothers did as well, and this can lead several generations of females to think, "Who needs fathers?" Studies have shown that a child needs a loving male presence when they are young. It doesn't necessarily have to be the biological father but, ideally, there is a loving man who is a constant presence in the child's life. For a girl baby, it is how she learns what safe love from a man feels like. Her daddy's (or uncle's or grandpa's) lap and arms are like a rehearsal space for appropriate male warmth and caring. Girls who are deprived of this can tend to search for male love in all the wrong places. Little boys need a male presence to show them how to be in the world. A father (or father figure) provides the blueprint for how to be a man and a father. Studies show that boys with involved fathers do better in school, especially in math and science. Naturally, we are speaking here of fathers who are responsible, kind, nurturing men, not violent or sexually abusive men.

Consequences for Boys

So what's the impact of teenage parenting on the father, you may ask. Again, studies have shown that young men who have children and then abandon them are more likely to turn to substance abuse to numb the psychic pain they experience. They may not even be aware of the source of their pain. But it is there, inside them. When such men are reunited with their child, it is possible that they will be motivated to turn their lives around, stop abusing drugs or alcohol, and try harder to find employment so as to provide child support. A wise man said to me once, "When you connect the father's heart to his child, his mind will follow."

Ways to Prevent Pregnancy

If you are thinking about having male-female sex, then it is time to think about what you and your partner are going to do to prevent pregnancy. Make an appointment to discuss contraception with your medical provider so you are all set before your first intercourse. This will reduce your anxiety about a possible pregnancy, and is the first step toward caring for yourself and your partner. Always use a condom in addition to whatever form of birth control you chose. You will greatly reduce your risk of contracting an STI.

Some kinds of contraception are more effective than others.

Here are some longer descriptions of the different methods of birth control available, listed in the order of their effectiveness:

The most effective forms are the ones that are long-lasting and do not require remembering every day or week. Implants such as Nexplanon are one type. Small matchstick-like rods are inserted, or implanted, under the surface of your skin, usually in the upper arm. They last for about three years. They can be removed at any time. This is a convenient type of contraception for a teenager who may not be interested in becoming pregnant for many years.

Another long-term contraceptive is the intrauterine device (IUD), such as Mirena, a small device that is introduced through the cervix and into the uterus by a doctor. IUDs can remain in place for three to ten years, depending on the type of IUD, and can also be removed anytime you would like to become pregnant. You are likely to experience a small amount of spotting while the IUD is in place, which may require wearing a panty liner.

The next most effective methods are shots, oral contraceptive pills ("the Pill"), patches, and rings. Depo-provera is an injection of contraception that is given every eleven to twelve weeks. It is very effective at preventing pregnancy if given properly every few months. Some teenagers who use Depo will have spotting (small amount of bleeding) or will stop having periods altogether during the time they are using it. You can become pregnant if you miss a shot.

Oral contraceptive pills are very popular and have been in use for many years. If you decide to use the Pill, you need to trust yourself to take it every day at about the same time. There are many different types of pills, and you and your provider or family planning counselor can decide together which one would be best for you.

A contraceptive patch is a small patch that you place on your skin. It contains the same hormones that pills contain. You put the patch on your skin once a week for three weeks, then take a week off. During the week off, you will have a menstrual period. The following week you start again.

The Nuvaring is a small ring that you insert deep into your vagina. It stays in place for three weeks. You then remove it and leave it out for one week, during which time you will get your period. The following week you put in a new one. Nuvarings also contain the same hormones that are in the pill, but you only need to use it once monthly. You must feel comfortable inserting something into your vagina in order to use the Nuvaring. Once in place, you cannot feel it, and it cannot get lost.

Every sexually active young woman should have access to Plan B. Plan B is a pill that can prevent pregnancy after unprotected sex. It comes in either one- or two-pill dosages, and it must be taken within 72 hours of having unprotected sex. If you are under the age of 17, you must have a prescription. Ask for a prescription at your next doctor appointment.

Choosing which contraceptive is right for you is a very personal decision. Think about your privacy (do you need to keep your method a secret from your parents? your partner?), the likelihood you would remember a daily pill, how comfortable you are inserting things into your vagina, how you would feel about not having a period. Knowing these things will help you decide the best method for you. Planned Parenthood has a questionnaire on their website to help you think about it before you see your provider. See in Resources at the end of this chapter.

Since the two of you are having sex, both of you should be doing something to prevent pregnancy. If you share sex, share the responsibility. That means the female chooses a method—implant, IUD, pill, patch, or injectable—and the male wears a condom. This approach can also help prevent STIs, which will be discussed in Chapter 14.

Male Condoms

Male condoms are cheap and easy to buy in drugstores, grocery stores, and convenience stores. A condom is a soft cover made of a very thin, rubbery material called latex; latex gives condoms their nickname, "rubbers."

Here is how to use a male condom properly:

- Use a new condom with every act of sexual intercourse, from start to finish.
- Use only latex or polyurethane condoms. Animal-skin condoms do not provide any protection against sexually transmitted diseases.
- Store condoms in a cool place out of direct sunlight and not in a wallet or glove compartment. Do not use damaged, discolored, brittle, or sticky condoms.
- Check the expiration date on the package.
- Carefully open the condom package. Teeth and fingernails can tear a condom. If a condom rips or tears, take out another one. It is a good idea to have several condoms on hand.

- Put on a condom after the penis is erect and before it touches your partner's body. If a penis is uncircumcised, pull back the foreskin before putting on the condom.
- Unroll the condom a little bit to make sure that it is being unrolled in the right direction. The rolled ring should be on the outside. If the condom doesn't unroll easily on the penis it is probably on upside down. Throw it away and begin again.
- If you need additional lubrication, use a condom lubricated with spermicide or a water-based lubricant like Astroglide (available at pharmacies). Other lubricants such as Vaseline, cooking oil, baby oil, or hand lotion will weaken the condom.
- Put on the condom by pinching the reservoir tip (the space at the end of the condom that will collect the semen) and unrolling it all the way down the shaft of the penis from the head to the base. If a condom does not have a reservoir tip, leave a half-inch space at the head of the penis for the semen to collect after ejaculation.
- Very soon after ejaculation and before the penis becomes soft again, withdraw the penis, holding on to the condom at the base to prevent slippage and leakage.
- Wrap the used condom in tissue and discard it in a wastebasket. Do not flush condoms in the toilet or leave them on the ground.

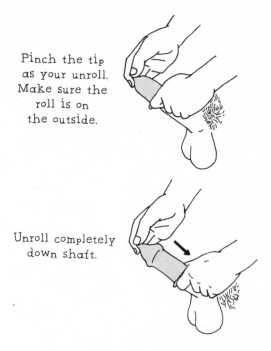

Pinch the tip as your unroll. Make sure the roll is on the outside.

Unroll completely down shaft.

How to Put on a Condom

Some Boys Don't Want to Use a Condom

Some males will argue against the use of a condom, saying it is less spontaneous, reduces sensation, and is costly or embarrassing to buy. None of these are legitimate reasons to go without protection. People who do not practice safe sex are denying the truth that anyone can get sick from STIs. Using a condom is not about how much you love or trust someone—it is about safety. Think of it as common sense—like wearing a seat belt in a car or a helmet when you go biking or skateboarding. Any man who refuses to wear a condom isn't the type of man you want to be having sex with. If you want to have sex, it has to be safe, and on your terms.

Myths About Preventing Pregnancy

A woman can still get pregnant:
- whether or not she has an orgasm.
- if the male has any semen on his finger and puts it into her vagina.
- if she has vaginal intercourse while standing, if she is bleeding from her vagina when she has sex, or if she has not even begun to menstruate.
- if it's her first time.
- if she jumps up and down right after sex. The sperm will not come out.
- if she douches, showers, or washes right after sex.
- if she's been having sex for a while and hasn't gotten pregnant the other times.
- if the man pulls out before he ejaculates. This is known as the withdrawal method.

Using withdrawal as a method of contraception is not suggested. Pulling out poses a risk because during intercourse, a clear fluid (also sometimes called pre-cum) comes out the end of the penis, and this fluid may contain sperm if there is some left behind from a previous recent ejaculation. (Pre-ejaculate does not contain sperm on its own but there is a small chance leftover sperm could become mixed in.) It is safest to not take any chances. Do not rely on the man pulling out before he ejaculates.

If You Become Pregnant

Each pregnant teen has three options with her pregnancy.

Becoming a Parent

She can choose to continue the pregnancy and become a parent. For teens who plan to continue a pregnancy and become parents, start prenatal care: take a prenatal vitamin and stop smoking, drinking, or doing any drugs. Discuss with your partner and both of your families how you are going to move forward. Discuss things like housing, work, money, education.

Adoption

She can choose to continue the pregnancy and seek adoption services. For teens who plan to continue a pregnancy and adopt, do all of the above, but also ask a doctor if he or she knows a social worker who can help you set up an adoption.

Abortion

She can end the pregnancy and seek abortion services. Remember that if you have Plan B and have had unprotected intercourse in the previous seventy-two hours (three days), take your Plan B. It works by preventing implantation of a fertilized egg into the wall of the uterus.

For teens who need to end a pregnancy, there are options

for abortion care. If the pregnancy is less than nine weeks, a medication abortion can be accomplished by using the medicine RU-486. This can come only from a doctor who is familiar with prescribing this medicine. A woman using medication abortion will experience cramping and bleeding, much like a spontaneous miscarriage at home. If she is more than nine weeks pregnant, or prefers not to take the pills, a woman can have a surgical abortion, with a D&E (dilation & evacuation) or with a D&C (dilation and curettage). These are simple procedures done most often in a clinic setting. They are virtually the same. For a D&C, the cervix (opening to the uterus) is dilated or stretched open about a centimeter. Then a curette is used to scrape the wall of the uterus to remove the pregnancy. An evacuation is when a small suction device is used to vacuum out the contents of the uterus. Often an abortion includes both curettage and evacuation. Both approaches to abortion are very safe and do not interfere with your future ability to get pregnant.

When Is Talking to a Professional Confidential?

If you think you cannot discuss these issues with your parents, some states allow teens to discuss contraception, adoption, or abortion with a doctor confidentially. Your health information is generally considered "privileged" and "protected," based on federal law.

Still, it is important for you to understand what doctors and mental health professionals cannot keep private.

When Is It Not Confidential?

First of all, professionals can never keep it a secret if a person under eighteen is being abused in any way. If the pregnancy is the result of statutory rape or incest, the physician must report it to the authorities because the law has been violated. Statutory rape is when an older boy or man has sex with a young woman who is not legally able to give consent. The age at which you can give consent varies from one state to another.

Whether you are old enough to see a doctor by yourself depends on the laws in your state. Many states allow minors to consent to their own medical care as it relates to reproductive health and birth control. In most states, if you are seeking birth control, you are considered an "emancipated minor" and allowed to give consent for your own care. Your own doctor should be able to provide this care for you, but some doctors refer teenagers to family planning clinics, like Planned Parenthood, for their reproductive health care. However, your ability to independently fill prescriptions or get medical procedures (including abortions) varies from state to state. If you are not sure about what medical care you need, and talking to your parents about it is not an option, you can call a doctor's office without giving your name and ask about options for someone your age. You could also call the hotline at Planned Parenthood (1–800–230–PLAN) for advice.

Planned Parenthood has clinics all over the country for males and females. Their services are low-cost and sometimes free.

Resources

- Planned Parenthood: 434 West 33rd Street, New York, NY 10001 1–800–230–PLAN
  www.plannedparenthood.org
- Go Ask Alice!: A question-and-answer website affiliated with Columbia University
  www.goaskalice.columbia.edu
- National Council for Adoption: 225 N. Washington Street, Arington, VA 22314; 1–703–299–6633
  www.adoptioncouncil.org
- National Adoption Information Clearinghouse: P.O. Box 1182, Washington, D.C. 20013; 1–703–352–3488 or 1–888–251–0075
  www.adoption.org
- Adoption Institute
  www.adoptioninstitute.org/research/domestic adoption.php
- Sex in the States, from Sex, Etc.: This website for teens provides state-by-state information about rights to sex education, birth control, access to abortion, and more.
  www.sexetc.org/state

14.

Sexually Transmitted Infections

How Do You Get an STI?

Any act of sex (oral, anal, vaginal) can lead to a sexually transmitted infection (STI or STD) for either partner.

How are you going to keep each other safe? Using condoms every time is the most effective way to prevent STIs. As I have said before, if you or your partner have been sexually active already, you will need to get tested. Do not accept anyone's word that he or she is free of an STI.

Some STIs are inconvenient and curable; others are painful and permanent. By choosing to have sex, you and your partner are linking yourselves together. You are linking together your health. People in caring relationships make certain that they keep their partners safe and healthy.

Some Basic Facts About STIs

- STIs vary. Some are serious diseases that can cause infertility in adults and birth defects in babies. Some STIs can lead to chronic health problems.
- Some STIs are curable, but others aren't.
- You can get the same STIs over and over again.
- Some STIs can be passed from a pregnant female to her baby during birth or afterward through her breast milk.
- Sometimes STIs don't cause symptoms, or one STI can cause the same symptoms as another one, or they can be mistaken for flu symptoms. A doctor's test can find out for sure.
- You can get or give STIs through oral, anal, and vaginal sex.
- You can get STIs not only from sexual contact with an infected person, but also by touching his or her sores, blisters, bumps, warts, mucous membranes, or skin.
- People also pass on some STIs by sharing infected drug needles or syringes, tattoo needles, body-piercing needles or jewelry, razors, manicure or pedicure instruments—any type of instrument that can cut, scrape, or enter the body.

What If You Contract an STI?

Most STIs don't cause symptoms, meaning that anyone can have them and not know. This also means that people with STIs look just the same as people without STIs. If you are having a symptom (pain, fever, genital sores or bumps, vaginal discharge, penile discharge, or pain with peeing), see a doctor and take your partner with you. If you have an STD, it is your job to make sure your partner is safe, too.

You should be tested once a year, or any time you begin a relationship with a new partner. Testing for the most common STIs is as simple as giving a urine specimen in a cup.

The Most Common STIs

STIs can be caused by bacteria or viruses. In general, bacterial infections can be treated and cured with antibiotics, while viral infections cannot be and can turn into chronic conditions that require ongoing care.

Bacterial Infections

Chlamydia:
Chlamydia is by far the most common and occurs in high rates in teenagers. You may have no symptoms at all or it may cause vaginal bleeding when you do not have a period, increased vaginal discharge, pain or burning with urination, or a discharge from the penis in boys or men. Repeated infections with chlamydia can affect your fertility in the future.

It is curable with antibiotics. After treatment most doctors will have you come back for "test of cure" to be sure you are free of chlamydia. It is important that your partner is treated at the same time, or you will become re-infected. As with all STIs the best way to prevent chlamydia is to use condoms.

Gonorrhea:

Gonorrhea may cause a green or brown discharge, vaginal bleeding, pain deep in the pelvis, or no symptoms at all. It can infect other parts of the body through the bloodstream, like your joints. Oral sex with a partner infected with gonorrhea can cause a throat infection with gonorrhea. Gonorrhea can be passed on to an infant during the birth process, so all pregnant women are screened for gonorrhea during pregnancy. It is treatable with antibiotics. You and your partner should be treated at the same time. Antibiotics such as penicillin G, ceftriaxone, and doxycycline are preferred treatments.

Syphilis:

Syphilis is the most serious and dangerous of the bacterial STIs. Early symptoms, lasting six to ten weeks, can include severe pain, a painless sore called a *chancre*[1] and enlarged lymph nodes close to the chancre. The illness can then have a latent period, where no symptoms are observed. During the second phase of the infection, symptoms include a rash. In the last phase of the illness, the infection attacks the nervous system and other organs. Although rare, this can lead to incurable mental illness, paralysis, and severe pain.

---

[1]   chancre (**shan**-ker)

Syphilis is curable with antibiotics such as penicillin. Safe-sex practices are helpful for reducing the odds of transmission, but the disease can still be passed through mucous membranes or chancres during touching and foreplay.

Viral Infections

Although they can be treated to help relieve the symptoms, viral STIs are not curable.

Human Papillomavirus (HPV) (also called genital warts):

Causes very contagious warts outside or inside the genitals and in the throat. The warts are most dangerous on a female's cervix because they can cause cervical cancer. A vaccine to prevent HPV, approved in 2006, is now widely available for both boys and girls. It requires three shots over the course of about six months, and is extremely effective in preventing genital warts.

Hepatitis:

The viral types of hepatitis, A, B, and C, can be passed on through sexual contact, are very contagious, and can cause liver cancer and death. You can get hepatitis A also from food and water, and types B and C from syringes and needles. Types A and B can be prevented by vaccination, but there's no vaccine for type C. You have most likely received a vaccine against hepatitis B, which has been given to all infants in the United States for over twenty years.

Hepatitis B is transmitted most commonly through sexual contact. It is more contagious than HIV/AIDS because it can be passed along in saliva through kissing or sharing toothbrushes. It can result in a yellowing of the skin and eyes, accompanied by fever and/or nausea. Often there are no observable symptoms.

Herpes Simplex Virus (HSV):

HSV is very common because in most people it causes mild or no symptoms, so they don't know that they have it and can pass it on. In other people, herpes causes repeated outbreaks of tiny, painful blisters at times of physical and emotional stress. These break open and release fluid that's very contagious when touched. Herpes blisters can appear on the face (even in the eyes or mouth) or anywhere else on the body, including on or inside the genitals. The sores can be treated with medicine to make the virus retreat inside the body so that they heal faster, but there's no cure, and the virus can become active again. Typically, cold sores around the mouth are associated with HSV-1 and genital outbreaks are associated with HSV-2.

If you become pregnant, it is very important to let your medical provider know if you have been infected with HSV, because the risk to a newborn is very serious. If a woman has active blisters at the time of delivery, the baby will be delivered by cesarean section to prevent infection in the baby.

Human Immunodeficiency Virus (HIV):

The fastest growing group of people infected with HIV, the virus that causes AIDS, are young people aged fifteen to twenty-four.

Human immunodeficiency virus (HIV) causes *acquired immunodeficiency syndrome* (AIDS). People can be *HIV-positive*—infected with the virus—for more than ten years before any symptoms appear and they learn that they can give it to others. By taking special combinations of medicines, people can maintain a healthy life without it developing into AIDS.

If you are HIV positive, you will need to have a long-term relationship with a doctor who specializes in HIV. You will take daily medicines and have your blood checked periodically. Many HIV-positive people now live very long lives, with the virus not even detectable in their blood as long as they take their medicines.

AIDS:

AIDS is the most dangerous STI because it destroys the body's ability to protect itself against infections. This is why AIDS causes so many different symptoms as the people who have it become extremely sick and die.

Because AIDS is deadly, people worry about whether they can get it just from being around HIV-positive people or from touching them or something that they touched. But HIV is not passed along by casual contact. HIV is transmitted *only* through infected body fluids and instruments that have become contaminated with them.

This is how you can contract HIV:

- from infected semen or vaginal fluid that enters your body during unprotected vaginal, oral, or anal intercourse. The fragile membranes in the vagina, mouth, and rectum can absorb the virus and do so more quickly if irritated or torn during intercourse.
- from infected blood that gets into your bloodstream through a skin opening, your mucous

membranes, or your eyes, or on an instrument that
can pierce or cut the skin
- from breast milk from an HIV-positive female
- HIV can also be passed from a pregnant female to
  her baby during birth, unless she takes medicines
  to prevent it. For this reason all pregnant women
  are screened for HIV during pregnancy and are
  treated with medicine if they are positive.

Scientists first became aware of AIDS in the 1980s, when
many gay men began developing the illness. This caused AIDS
to become associated with homosexuality even though anybody can contract HIV.

15.

Sexual Abuse

Experiencing sexual abuse of any kind affects your self-esteem, your ability to trust and to have successful relationships, your behavior, and how you feel about your body. It can affect your very identity!

It's important for you to understand what sexual abuse is and, if you have been a victim or know someone who has been a victim, what you can do about it. Both boys and girls can experience sexual abuse and unwanted sexual touching. One in four girls and one in six boys are victims. And 90 percent are victimized by someone the family knows and trusts.

What Is Sexual Abuse?

Sexual abuse is forcing you into any kind of unwanted sexual activity. This includes someone touching you sexually, showing you his or her genitals, showing you sexual pictures, or doing anything else sexual. Sexual abuse is against the law, and nobody—*nobody*—has the right ever to do it.

You can be sexually abused in all kinds of ways, all of which are illegal, even if it happens one time.

If You Are Sexually Abused

If you yourself have been a victim of sexual abuse, you probably know how hard it is to talk about what happened. But it is really important to talk about it, especially with an adult who is compassionate, understanding, and will believe you. There are people specially trained to help you if you're being or have been abused. Breaking the wall of silence and telling someone is the first step to healing . . . provided they believe you.

The good news is that there are many resources you can turn to for help, and I list them later on in this chapter. With the support of friends, family, and professionals, it is possible to overcome the effects of sexual abuse and go on to feel good about yourself and your relationships.

It Is Never Your Fault

Being sexually abused is never your fault. No matter what happens, or how it happens, or how often, or who else is involved, it's never your fault. You're not to blame for it:

- not even if you said yes,
- not even if it felt good,
- not even if it happened more than once, over months or years.

Types of Sexual Abuse

Sexual Harassment

Sexual harassment is when a person bothers you repeatedly with sexual attention that you don't want and that makes you uncomfortable. The federal government says that sexual harassment takes two forms:

1. Making you have sexual contact to avoid a threat or to get a benefit like a better grade or a position on a sports team.
2. Making you feel uncomfortable in any of these ways:
   - commenting on your sexuality by criticizing, complimenting, whistling, catcalling, or engaging in unwelcome flirting
   - spreading sexual rumors
   - flashing
   - groping, unwanted touching

- leaving sexual graffiti on your locker or on your Facebook page
- making general sexual remarks to you or telling sexual jokes without your consent
- wondering out loud if you're gay, accusing you of being gay, or hounding gay people
- suggesting that you have sex of any kind
- showing you or sending you sexual pictures

All of the above are examples of clear-cut harassment and are illegal. You have the right to state clearly that you do not want it to continue and that, if it does, you will report the person to someone in authority.

You can also write a letter to the person, describing the behavior and saying you want it to stop, otherwise you will report them. Put a date on the letter and keep a copy. Written documents can be important for fighting harassment. Keep a journal as well, or try to keep a log of what types of incidents happened, who was involved, what you said, and how it was handled by the school or employer. This will give you credibility if you need to press charges. Remember—if you alert your school (or employer, if you have a job) that you are being harassed and they fail to stop the harassment, they are not following the law. Sexual teasing at school that continues after a student has complained about it to school administrators could be grounds for a lawsuit.

Molestation

Molestation is direct, unwanted sexual contact with a child or teenager. It is against the law.

Molesters try to confuse you. They may give you gifts or take you exciting places. They may try to act like your friend or mentor. They know that you have probably been taught to respect and obey adults, so they try to use that authority to make you do sexual things. Or the molester may be someone you love, and if the sexual behavior is gentle and loving rather than hurtful, it's confusing to know that it's wrong. You can be bothered, embarrassed, or frightened by a harasser or stalker who never even comes near you. If your abuser uses threats to try to get his or her way, *it's still abuse, even if you refuse.*

Incest

Incest is sexual activity among family members and children or teenagers. The person can be a parent, grandparent, aunt or uncle, cousin, sister, or brother. This, too, is illegal.

Often a victim of incest will be told that what is happening is normal and he or she may not realize that it is a form of abuse. The abuser may have threatened the victim. The victim may not know that there is help available; he or she may be scared of what will happen if he or she tells someone and he or she may be ashamed, or afraid of not being believed, or afraid that the person he or she confides in will tell the abuser.

If the abuser is a parent, sometimes the nonabusing parent will not believe it when told about the abuse. Sometimes the nonabusing parent is aware of the abuse and chooses—for whatever reason—not to take action to stop it.

There are many reasons that a nonabusing parent might not stop the abuse, including that he or she may be dependent on the abuser for shelter or income and thus think that allowing the incest to continue is the only way to keep his or her partner.

By the way, when children are very young it is not unusual for young boys and girls to be curious and want to explore one another's bodies. This childhood play is not the same as incest. I remember "playing doctor" with my girl and boy cousins of the same age when we were seven or eight, but we soon grew out of it.

Assault or Rape

Sexual assault is forced sexual contact, including touching someone's breasts, buttocks, or genitals, even if intercourse does not happen. It is illegal.

Rape is sexual intercourse that takes place either against someone's will or when he or she is unconscious or under the influence of alcohol or drugs.

Acquaintance or *date rape* involves a date or a friend. It is important to be clear about what date rape is. If someone gives you a clear message to stop touching him or her, and you continue anyway, you have assaulted him or her. If you penetrate someone sexually after he or she told you not to, it is rape.

Alcohol is often involved in date rapes and sexual assaults. The victim may be spaced out on drugs or drunk. Someone who is drunk or drugged and cannot make a clearheaded decision to consent to sex has been date-raped. Rates of date rape are especially high among seniors in high school and freshmen in college.

Some perpetrators try to drug victims with powerful sedatives called "roofies" (Rohypnol), which are more powerful than other tranquilizers like Valium. This drug is illegal in the

United States, but it is legal in some countries in Europe and Latin America. If a person unknowingly swallows this drug, it can make him or her feel paralyzed, have the spins, get blurred vision, or feel as if he or she is in a dream. The drug is so powerful that the victim may not even retain a memory of the assault experience. This is why Rohypnol and similar drugs have become known as date-rape drugs. This is why you should never drink a punch or any drink that has been mixed out of your sight. If you have a drink, watch it being made or watch a bottle being opened.

Even if you are romantically interested in a person, you must not push them further sexually than they are willing to go. It is very common when you begin dating for you to want to kiss or touch a person, but not move on to sex immediately. This is the right way to build a physical relationship. If you start out kissing or touching, you or your partner are allowed to stop anytime you want to. Your direction to stop must be respected by your partner. No one has a right to "just go a little further" without your say-so.

And you need to know that a physical attack like rape can cause not only physical and emotional wounds but also pregnancy and sexually transmitted diseases (STDs), including HIV/AIDS.

Trust Your Feelings

Usually young people can tell if another person is trying to start something weird. If any person or situation makes you feel strange or uncomfortable in any way, pay attention. Get away quickly. Don't try to tell yourself—and don't let anyone else tell you—that you're imagining things. Even if nothing happens and you just walk away, tell one or both parents, or another adult you trust, how you felt. You don't have to explain why—you may not even know—but you do need to speak up and say that the person made you feel creepy.

No one should ever be made to have sex if he or she doesn't want to. No one—not a mother, father, grandparent, uncle, brother, cousin, neighbor, teacher, minister, rabbi, coach, baby-sitter, boyfriend, girlfriend, or stranger—has the right to force you to engage in any sexual activity or to harass you sexually.

Saying "No"

Don't ever be afraid to say "NO!" or "STOP!" Yell it if you have to.

When it comes to sex, the word "Yes" means "Just this once." Each time anyone wants sexual contact, he or she needs the other person's consent. Even if two people already have a sexual relationship, either one can always say "no" to sexual contact at any time.

If You Have Been Molested

The molester will often tell the victim all kinds of lies to keep him or her quiet. Here are some of the common lies victims hear, followed by the truth:

Lie: "You can't tell, because you already promised not to."

Truth: Go ahead and promise whatever a molester wants so that you can get away. A molester is a sick criminal, and there's no reason to keep your promise to an abuser.

Lie: "If you tell, I'll hurt you, or your family or friends, or I'll kill your pets."

Truth: Tell right away! The police and child authorities will help.

Lie: "We share a special love," or "You're my best friend, and friends don't tell on each other."

Truth: A person who loves you or is really your friend wants to protect you from any harm, including sexual abuse. No matter how much you love the person who molested you, there's always someone you must love more—yourself.

Lie: "If you tell, people will blame you for what happened."

Truth: Most people, and all counselors, know that young people who have been sexually abused are afraid of being blamed and that they are never to blame.

Lie: "If you tell, nobody will believe you."

Truth: Most people, and all counselors, know that it's hard for kids to tell about sexual abuse and that it's rare that they lie about it. Some people may not believe you, especially if you tell a family member that another relative abused you. Right away go tell another adult whom you trust, or call 911. Keep telling as many adults as you can.

Lie (if it's incest): "If you tell, it will break up our family, and you'll have to go to an orphanage."

Truth: Your family is already broken. You'll help the whole family by telling, so that they can get help.

Lie: "If you tell, I'll be locked up in jail."

Truth: Although a molester has broken the law, a judge might decide instead to require him or her to get counseling. But even if the molester is not locked up, you'll be protected.

Lie: "We have been doing this for a long time, so people will know that you wanted it to happen."

Truth: Most people, and all counselors, know that sexual abuse can continue for years just because the victim can't defend him- or herself.

If You Have Been Raped or Assaulted

If you are raped, there are some practical things you will need to do. You will need to talk with professionals who can tell you how to protect your health and press charges against the attacker. Here are the most important things to remember:

- Do not bathe, wash, or get rid of soiled clothing. Your body and clothes provide important pieces of physical evidence.
- Tell someone—the police, a doctor, or a hotline worker.
- Get to a hospital or a clinic. You should get the "rape kit" procedure, which is a medical examination conducted by a person specifically trained to collect evidence of rape. If you only feel comfortable with a woman examining you, you can request it. If a female physician is not available you can request that a second medical professional (like a nurse) also be present in order for you to feel safe.

- You can expect to talk with a counselor or arrange follow-up counseling at the hospital.
- During the next few weeks you will need to get tested for sexually transmitted diseases and pregnancy. Roughly six months after your attack you will want to be tested for HIV.
- You should consider joining a sexual-assault survivors group to help you heal emotionally.

If You Don't Tell

Keeping silent about sexual abuse can have consequences:
- If you don't tell someone that you were molested, your whole life and everything you do may possibly be affected by this terrible secret. People have come forward ten, twenty, even thirty or more years after they were abused and told tragic stories about how suffering in silence damaged their lives.
- Telling is important if you are to get the help and the support you need and deserve.
- There's a limited amount of time during which a molester can be punished for his or her crime. If you wait too long to tell, your assailant might never be punished.
- Not telling leaves the molester free to attack other kids just as he or she did you.

This is why you must also tell if you know another child, perhaps a friend, who has been abused—even if he or she made you promise to keep the secret. This is hard to do, but after having been helped to get better, he or she will understand how strong you were to do the right thing.

Effects of Childhood Sexual Abuse

If you were abused when you were little, you are not alone. You should not feel like a broken person because of the experience. It is possible that you would want to withdraw from the world of dating. These responses are understandable. But they can often get in the way of happy and healthy relationships. It is important to keep appropriate boundaries, to say no to casual sex with unfamiliar partners. You don't want to add to your memories of abuse with negative sexual experiences today.

People who have been sexually abused respond in different ways. Some victims recover relatively quickly, others may go on to feel depressed, fearful, dirty, self-hating, or even suicidal for some time after the experience. Some try to numb their pain by cutting themselves.

If you were abused in childhood, it could be confusing for you to move ahead with new romantic relationships, even with a loving and trustworthy partner. Sexual touching can bring up a mix of conflicting feelings for those who were abused as children, including fear, anger, or physical pleasure interspersed with guilt.

If your abuse was repeated over and over again, you may have developed mental habits that helped you cope with the abuse—such as feeling disconnected from your body, numb, or dissociated from your surroundings. If you have ever experienced these feelings, it does not mean you are crazy. It's a sign that you found a mental strategy to help you escape your situation. You are resourceful.

But to heal from your pain you need to get help from an individual who is trained in dealing with victims of sexual abuse.

Resources

If you want to tell an adult you know personally but you can't tell a parent, you can go to a teacher, school nurse, doctor, religious leader, relative, or family friend. Here are hotlines that help victims of sexual abuse, assault, and incest:

> National Child Abuse Hotline: 1–800–4–A-CHILD
> (1–800–422–4453)
> National Coalition Against Sexual Assault:
> 1–717–728–9764; email: ncasa@redrose.net
> Rape, Abuse, and Incest National Network (RAINN)
> www.rainn.org
> National Sexual Assault Hotline, a service of RAINN:
> 1–800–656–HOPE(4673)

. . . or call 911 and tell the police.

The National Sexual Assault Hotline is a free, confidential service. A live person will provide help over the RAINN website to victims of sexual assault or friends of victims. It works just like instant messaging. You'll go into a private session with a trained volunteer and communicate, live, by typing messages back and forth. The service is completely anonymous, and you do not have to give your name or any personal information. You will receive referrals to resources in your area, information on what to expect when you report the crime to the police, answers to your questions about recovering from sexual assault, and more.

In most cases, people will be sympathetic to you if you disclose that you were sexually assaulted. If you are met with an insensitive response, you can keep the following things in mind:

- Being assaulted was not your fault, even if you had been friendly to your attacker.
- Your body, looks, or clothes did not cause or excuse the sexual assault.
- The attack does not reflect on you or your character—it reflects only on the attacker.
- Thinking of the experience simply as an act of violence, and not a sexual experience, may make it easier to discuss with others.

I also suggest you have a parent get in touch with Safe Horizons, a victims' assistance group that operates in several child-advocacy centers in New York City and at the Childhood Violent Trauma Clinic at Yale University. Safe Horizons has developed a proven (and brief) therapy program for victims and their family members, Call 1–203–785–2540 (Yale Center) or 1–212–227–3000 (New York Center) www.safehorizon.org

IV

Important Relationships

16.

Family

Families can come in all shapes and sizes. Children may live with one or both biological parents, adoptive parents, stepparents, foster parents, grandparents, or other adult caregivers. They may have two mothers or two fathers or one of each. If anyone teases you about the way your family is, just know that what matters is that there is love. Even if you don't feel there is love in your family, you are strong, and you can get through it by trying to know who you are and being true to yourself. As you go through life, you will find love in many forms and that will make you even stronger.

Independence

Because of all the changes that go on during puberty and adolescence, there can be more disagreements among family members at that time. There can be a tug-of-war between your need for independence and your need for connection, between being your own person and being intimate with people you care about. You may want more independence, and this may stress your parents.

You might feel like everything is wrong with your parents. It was probably during middle school that you started to want more of your own space and privacy. Your brother or sister bugged you more than before. These feelings can create tension and you may find that there's more fighting going on between you and family members. You have begun to realize that your parents are not perfect. No, they're not, and no one else is, either. It can seem as if parents don't want you to grow up, or don't hear what you're trying to tell them.

Understanding Your Parents

You may not always agree with your parents, but try to understand that they are doing the best they can. Parents tend to worry. You may think they worry too much. Part of what's confusing about puberty and adolescence is that one minute you think that they just don't understand and should leave you alone and the next minute you want them to put their arms around you and hold you.

It's not always easy to talk to your parents—especially about personal issues like romance, dating, and sex. If you have a girlfriend or boyfriend you may feel strongly about your privacy and not want your parents to know every detail about your social life. Nonetheless, parents and other family members can often provide guidance. You may need your parents' cooperation if you are in a tough situation.

Some adults find it hard to talk about sex. They might become embarrassed when it's time to be direct. It's not easy for parents to recognize your new thoughts and feelings. But your parents have had lots of experiences and perhaps can be helpful sources of information. Your friends may give you wrong information.

Try to maintain an honest relationship with your parents. Think about how you want to set up a conversation about something important, such as sex. Give your parents a clear message that you have something meaningful to talk about and that you want their support. Don't just drop hints and hope they get the point. Instead, tell them that you have something important to discuss and you need them to be good listeners. You may have a better chance of creating a helpful and productive dialogue with your parents.

If, for any reason, you don't feel right talking with your parents about your body and your feelings, find another adult—another relative, your doctor, teacher, coach, or religious leader. Don't rely just on what your friends tell you. Or the Internet. They may not have the right answers.

Values

Parents can teach you values, and values are very important in life. Values are the strong feelings and beliefs that may guide you throughout your life. Values help you decide how to act in certain situations, how to treat people, what kinds of friends you make. People who live according to their values usually feel better about themselves. People who go against their values often experience guilt and feel bad.

17.

Friends

When you were younger, it was your family who played the biggest role in shaping your identity. Now it is your peers who influence how you make decisions and define yourself. Friends—whether you have them or wish you had them—become a central part of your life.

Choosing Your Friends

Back in Chapter 2, I asked you to think about the kind of person you want to be. The friends you choose now can help you become that person if they share your values, or they can do the opposite and lead you down the wrong path. This might happen if you're trying to fit in with a certain group who appear to be "in" but engage in risky behaviors. Don't do anything you feel unsure about just to fit in. Ask yourself why you are doing something, and what you're afraid might happen if you don't. Stay true to yourself and ask yourself if your friends are really good influences on you:

- Do your friends reflect your values?
- Do they support you and make you feel good consistently?
- When they criticize you, do they do it constructively or do they tear you down?

Don't be surprised if your friends change over time—maybe many times. This is very common in middle and high school.

Maybe now is the time to make an effort to find people who are more like you, both girls and guys. Becoming involved in after-school activities—sports, school plays, community youth groups, or camping trips—are good ways to meet new friends.

Changing Friendships

During adolescence it's expected that friendships will change. Probably you've already experienced this—staying friends with some of your schoolmates and neighbors, drifting away from others, losing those who drift away from you, and making new ones.

Friendships change at this time for all kinds of reasons.

- Popularity may become more important to some kids.

- Interests change.
- Your friends may become interested in having girl-friends or boyfriends and you may not be ready for that.
- You may be jealous of a friend's new boyfriend or girlfriend because your friend cares less about spending time with you.
- Or the opposite might happen—you might feel new attraction for a special boy or girl before your best friend feels that way.
- You'll need to make new friends just to be able to talk about all your new feelings.
- Some people might think that your male or female friend is your boyfriend or girlfriend and tease you about it.
- People might tease one another to the point of being mean or picking fights.
- People may want to engage in high-risk behavior like drinking or using drugs.

Tips for Good Relationships: Communication Is Key

Here are a few tips about having a good relationship, whether it's with a friend or a boyfriend or girlfriend:

- It's best to be honest about how you feel. This doesn't mean blurting out things that may hurt the other person. But there are ways to tell the truth that are sensitive to the other person's feelings.
- One way to do that is to focus on your feelings,

making "I" statements rather "you" statements, which make assumptions about the other person. For instance, if you've been feeling that your friend is ignoring you, rather than accusing and saying, "You've been ignoring me," or "You don't like me anymore," it's better to speak from your truth and say, "I've been feeling kind of left out lately. Why do you think that is? Am I imagining things?" By staying with what you feel, the other person won't feel accused and be put on the defensive.

• If someone has said something that has hurt you, it's best not to attack that person. Instead, make it clear that the comment—not the person—hurt your feelings and explain why.

Confrontation

If the group you want to be part of is mean to you and isolates you, find other friends. I know that it can be hard to get out of relationships that are abusive. You convince yourself to stay because they are nice to you sometimes. But you deserve to have true friends who help you feel good consistently, friends you can have fun with.

Try choosing one person in the group you feel the most comfortable with and consider telling him or her you know what is going on, that it hurts you, and you'd rather find other friends. This is much better than trying to stifle your feelings and pretending everything is just fine. You can make your true self stronger by staying with the truth.

But as you mature, it is also important to understand that almost all relationships are messy sometimes. Conflict is normal in life. Confrontation, as long as it is nonviolent and not mean, can be a great way to clear the air—much healthier than pretending all is well. It is not your job to "make nice" if an honest confrontation is what's needed! By confrontation, I am talking about using honest, cooperative words.

I know it can be scary to confront "friends" who have been mean, especially for girls, because close friendships are what adolescent girls' lives are so much about. You're afraid you'll end up being alone. I remember when I finally got up the nerve to confront my best friend in high school because she was ganging up against me with another girl. I was so scared because I really didn't have many other close friends. She didn't speak to me for a week or so, but then we got back together again, and, in fact, our friendship was even stronger.

Here is something I have learned over my lifetime and through many relationships: Sometimes a relationship becomes stronger when two people have confronted each other with whatever the problem is and worked it through. I can't help thinking of the exercise equivalent: When you lift weights to make your muscles stronger, tiny, microscopic tears (rips so small you could see them only under a microscope) occur in the muscle fiber. It takes forty-eight hours for the tears to mend (which is why you should not work the same muscles two days in a row) and, when they mend, scar tissue forms and makes the muscle stronger than it was before. Love and friendship can work the same way—become stronger when disagreements have been talked through and resolved.

18.

Bullying

What Is Bullying?

Bullying is very different from having disagreements with your friends. Some people may not be nice—at least at this time in their lives. Maybe they don't feel good about themselves and are mean to others. These people sometimes become bullies. Maybe you have even been a bully.

Bullying says more about the bully than it does you. If you are bullied, it is *not* your fault. Bullies are people who need to feel powerful. Hurting someone else makes them feel in control.

There are many forms of bullying.

Girls' Bullying

Many girls want to appear nice, kind, caring, and never angry or violent, and that's partly why girls' bullying is more hidden than boys'. It can include backbiting, exclusion, ignoring, spreading rumors, name-calling, ganging up, or making subtle, put-down gestures. Teachers may not be aware of girls' bullying, and may not call them on it the way they do boys.

Girls may think that even if they are mad at a friend, they shouldn't come right out and say it, so they go behind the person's back instead. If this is something you have done, know that your friend can tell you're mad by the way you're behaving. This is probably even more hurtful than a good fight because she feels it but isn't supposed to trust her feelings.

Also, when you go behind someone's back, you usually let your feelings stew and boil until you wind up getting really upset and losing control.

Boys' Bullying

As I write about in Chapter 3, our culture's view of masculinity and its pressures can cause boys to repress their feelings. When there are conflicts between boys, this can lead to physical aggression toward each other and toward boys who are "different"—who don't fit the culture's "masculine" model. It's not that boys don't also engage in backbiting and gossip the way girls do, but they tend to act out their bullying physically more than girls do.

You Can Get Out of It!

Do not stay in a bullying relationship. Do not tolerate meanness. Don't stay because you think you can change the person. Staying in it can cause you to believe that friendship and abuse go together and, later, that love and abuse go together. That's not a pattern you want to continue.

It may not be easy to tell your parents about the bullying at school and how hurtful it is. You may be worried about what their reaction will be, that they might only make it worse. But speak up and discuss it. It may be necessary for them to make the school aware of the bullying. If, for whatever reason, a parent isn't available, go to a coach, another trusted adult family member, or a religious leader for their help.

Things to Remember About Bullying

- If you are being bullied, as I said, it is not your fault. It is not about you! It is about the bully him/herself.
- Never get into a fight with a bully. Stay calm. It may be hard, but try to joke about it. Bullies often don't pick on people who refuse to let it upset them.
- Make note of the exact time and place where the bullying incident happened, what form the bullying took, and if anyone else witnessed it.
- Bullying is serious. It can lead to the bully's expulsion from school. Bullies need to know this.
- Don't bully others, even if your friends are doing it.
- Report the bullying to an adult, either your parents, a teacher, or a school official. Give them details, including emails, and so forth. If there were witnesses to what happened, see if they will report the bullying instead of you.

Cyberbullying

Bullies may use websites, social networks, or cell phones to send or post texts or images meant to hurt, embarrass, and torment the target of their cruelty. It can include:

- being ignored, disrespected, insulted, and called names

- taking inappropriate photos when a person doesn't realize it and sending them around
- using texts or photos stored on your cell phone or computer to blackmail you, get you to do or say something you don't want to do or say. If you don't, the bully can send them—through multimedia messaging or uploading to a site like Facebook or YouTube—throughout your school, your neighborhood, your city, the entire world, even.
- making unwanted sexual advances
- posting unflattering or personal or nude photos of people
- sending mean or threatening messages to someone
- using social media, instant messages, chat rooms, and email to create made-up stories about a person and posting them

Cyberbullying may be coming from someone you know, a friend, someone from school, or from a chat room. It may come from an ex-boyfriend or ex-girlfriend or a stranger. It may not be physical, but cyberbullying can spread quickly and leave a long-lasting trail that can do terrible damage to both the person being bullied and the bully. You cannot ignore it. You must certainly avoid the particular website, chat room, or message board where you were harassed. And you must speak up! You may need your parents' or guardians' help to stop the cyberbully. You can take official action by contacting your Internet service provider (ISP). If you are receiving death threats, the bully may face criminal charges.

Electronic Dating Violence

Cyberbullying usually happens between people who do not like or want to be around each other. But sometimes bullies use emails, cell phones, and the Internet to harass and bully their romantic partners. It is wise not to give your password to your friends or romantic partners, and never allow them to pay your cell phone bill. Studies show that people who share their passwords with friends or romantic partners are almost three times as likely to be victims of electronic violence. (Sameer Hinduja, Ph.D., and Justin W. Patchin, Ph.D, "Electronic Dating Violence: A Brief Guide for Educators and Parents," 2011, Cyberbullying Research Center, www.cyber bullying.us.) You may feel certain you can trust these friends, but you never know, and, as I pointed out earlier, relationships in high school can change.

You may know someone who has been stalked, harassed, checked up on constantly, or threatened by a former friend or romantic partner. Sometimes a victim can receive thousands of calls and texts at all hours of the day and night—"Where are you?" "Who are you talking to?"—to the point where the victim may become afraid to answer his or her calls or emails. Someone who is paying your phone bill may feel he or she has the right to monitor who calls or texts you. Because you have your phone or iPad with you all the time, you may end up having nowhere to hide from this harassment. It's as if the cyberbully has an electronic leash attached to you.

Sexting

Never send a nude or partly nude photo or video of yourself or any sexual text to anyone! You may think it will remain between you and a current friend, but someone who you think is your girlfriend or boyfriend may get mad at you or want to brag about you, and send it to others, and it can go viral. It can ruin your reputation and embarrass you or make you seem really stupid. The photo can live forever on cell phones and even on social networking sites. The police may be called in, and there could be serious consequences. It could result in your having to move from where you and your family live, and even then, the damage may follow if people recognize you.

If someone sends you a sexually compromising photo of him- or herself or someone else, do not send it to anyone else. If you do, and the person in the picture or video is under eighteen, you may be arrested for dissemination of child pornography, which is a serious felony, and put in a juvenile detention center for up to nine months. In some parts of the country even those who *receive* the photos and those who *save* the photos can be charged with child pornography and, these days, adult jail is also a possibility—and for longer than nine months!

As one boy who was responsible for forwarding a nude photo his girlfriend had sent of herself said, "Not only does it hurt the people that are involved in the pictures you send, it can hurt your family and friends around you, the way they see you, the way you see yourself. The ways they feel about you. Them crying because of your mistakes." (Jan Hoffman, "A Girl's Nude Photo, and Altered Lives," *The New York Times*, March 26, 2011.)

Sexting may be going on all around you in music videos and elsewhere, but don't be foolish enough to engage in it yourself. Respect yourself and be smart. Remember, you can never take it back, or control who sees it. It will be out there forever.

What You Must Do if You Have Been Bullied

Some victims of cyberbullying are able to dismiss the bullies as merely stupid, pathetic people with nothing better to do with their lives. On the other hand, some people are scared, saddened, become depressed and anxious, and feel helpless and angry.

If you have been the victim of cyberbullying, here are things you must do:

- As with any form of bullying, tell someone—your parents, another trusted adult, a school official.
- Save the emails, text messages, or blogs as proof. Most email accounts now offer services that will automatically filter out messages from certain senders before they even reach you.

Resources

Here are some websites that can help you deal with bullying:

- StopBullying.gov: The official U.S. government website managed by the Department of Health and Human Services in partnership with the Department of Education and Department of Justice

for information and resources on how to prevent and stop bullying
www.stopbullying.gov

- Teenangels.org: an award-winning teen cybersafety group
www.teenangels.org

- National Bullying Prevention Center: Pacer Center's Teens Against Bullying
www.pacerteensagainstbullying.org

- Teen Line: a confidential telephone helpline for teenage callers. It operates every evening from 6:00 P.M. to 10:00 P.M. PST. If you have a problem or just want to talk with another teen who understands, then this is the right place for you! You can call them at 1–800–852–8336 or 1–310–855–HOPE(4673). It is toll-free from anywhere in California. Text them by texting TEEN to 839863. Teen Line also offers message boards, resources, and information.
www.teenlineonline.org

Cyberbullying Resources

- www.cyberbullying.org
- www.netsmartz411.org

- www.stopbullying.gov/topics/cyberbullying
- Facebook: Safety Centre for Teens: helpful information about how to be safe on Facebook
  www.facebook.com/safety/groups/teens
- A Thin Line: "an MTV campaign that was developed to [empower individuals] to identify, respond to, and stop the spread of digital abuse in their life and among their peers"
  www.athinline.org

LGBTQ Resources

- Gay, Lesbian & Straight Education Network (GLSEN)—
  www.glsen.org

- It Gets Better Project: thousands of videos submitted by people across the country to inspire and encourage LGBTQ youth who are struggling. You can watch videos at www.ItGetsBetterProject.com.

- The Trevor Project: The Trevor Project is determined to end suicide among LBGTQ youth by providing resources and a nationwide twenty-four-hour hotline. If you are considering suicide or need help, call 1–866–4–U–TREVOR (866–488–7386).
  www.thetrevorproject.org

Online Resources You Can Show Your Parents and Guardians

StopBullying.gov: (information for parents)
www.stopbullying.gov/what-you-can-do/parents
/index.html

Start Strong: Through this website or by calling
1–415–678–5500, your parents or teachers can
access the organization Start Strong: Building
Healthy Teen Relationships. They have a "Moving
from a Relationship Bystander to a Relationship
Upstander" workshop guide.
www.startstrongteens.org

- Striving to Reduce Youth Violence Everywhere
(STRYVE): "a national initiative led by the Centers for Disease Control and Prevention (CDC) to
prevent youth violence before it starts among
young people ages ten to twenty-four"
www.vetoviolence.cdc.gov/stryve

- NetSmartz411: the parents' and guardians' premier, online resource for answering questions
about Internet safety, computers, and the Web.
www.netsmartz411.org

- PBS Parents—Resources by Topic: Bullies
www.pbs.org/parents/itsmylife/resources/bullies.html

- Facebook: Family Safety Centre
www.facebook.com/safety

19.

Feelings About Your Looks and Your Body

The most important thing I have to say on this subject is that your value as a person is not determined by how you look. Your self-esteem should not be attached to what other people think you should look like. As you grow up, you will learn that character, loving relationships, and kindness are far more important than looks. Many famous and successful women and men were not beautiful or popular as adolescents and spent most of their time alone because they were rejected by their peers. Maybe it was this time alone that helped them develop the very things that were special about themselves.

Unfortunately, girls tend to obsess about their looks and bodies partly because our culture places such importance on women fitting into a certain image of beauty. But boys worry as well.

Everyone's Different

Adolescence can be a difficult time because not everyone's body changes at the same time and in the same ways and we may judge ourselves in comparison. There will be girls and boys who are much more developed and more physically mature than you. Or perhaps you have developed earlier than most. Older boys may come on to girls who have early breast development in ways that make the girls uncomfortable. This can make girls feel that their bodies are what matters the most about them. Larger, more physically developed boys may find that people treat them as more mature than they are and expect more of them.

Sooner or later everyone will have a mature body; developing at different rates is a normal part of puberty.

Being Full-Figured or Overweight

Some teens have full figures starting at puberty, and this may never change, and that's okay. Others are heavy during puberty and thin out as they grow. There is a difference between being full-figured and being overweight or obese. Obesity is a serious health problem that can begin in childhood and lead to many serious illnesses. I will discuss obesity in more detail in a moment.

The Media and Body Image

As I have explained, the media offers a narrow view of what beauty is. If you believe all that you see in the media, especially in the advertisements, you might become upset that you don't measure up. You might worry that you're getting fat, for example, when you're really just having a growth spurt in which your height needs to catch up to your weight. This might cause you to obsess about how you look. Just remember, most people don't look like the actors and models in the media and never will. In fact, often the models don't look like that, either. With computers, photographers can change (digitally alter) the model's body shape, make a male seem more buff, make a female thinner and bigger-breasted, with technical tricks and air-brushing.

It's important to remember that the media's goal is to make money, not to give us realistic, healthy images of bodies and behavior.

How to Stay Healthy

Healthy Foods and Drinks
The key thing isn't if you are thin or full-figured. The key is being healthy, and that means eating a healthy, balanced diet that includes fresh fruits, vegetables, lean protein, and whole grains. The things to stay away from are sugary, fatty foods. Fast foods are especially full of fat and sugar.

Calcium is important for your growing bones, so try to eat and drink calcium-rich ingredients that will provide about 1,300 milligrams of calcium daily. Here are some ideas:

- nonfat milk
- calcium-fortified soy milk
- calcium-fortified almond milk
- nonfat yogurt
- low-fat cheese
- calcium-fortified cereals
- calcium-fortified orange juice
- tofu
- broccoli
- kale
- green beans

The best drink of all is water—plain or sparkling. Water is very good for you. Try adding fruit juice to sparkling water. Stay away from sodas that are loaded with sugar. Sodas are bad for you because the ones with sugar are very fattening. Artificial sweeteners aren't good for you, either. Juices and other sugary beverages like vitamin water or iced tea are also very high in calories. It's much healthier to eat an apple than it is to drink apple juice.

It's best not to drink too much caffeine (many sodas, energy drinks, and coffee contain it) because it can keep you from sleeping, and if you don't sleep enough, it affects your mood and ability to concentrate.

Tips for Healthy Eating

1. Eat breakfast. A healthy one is oatmeal, a whole-grain, non-fat or low-sugar cereal, whole-grain bread, and fresh fruit. Cut back on bacon and sausage or other processed, sugary foods. Include a source of protein, such as milk with your oatmeal, an egg, or a small amount of cheese, yogurt, or peanut butter.

2. Stick healthy snacks into your lunch box or locker—fruit and string cheese are good examples.

3. Make sure you've eaten a variety of colors before the day is over, especially the healthiest super foods that are dark green, blue/purple, and yellow/orange, like blueberries, red or orange peppers, carrots, broccoli, or kale. Deeply colored foods are higher in nutrients.

4. Make sure at least half of the food on your plate consists of fruits and/or veggies.

5. Learn to eat slowly and chew well.

6. Eat sitting down.

7. Focus on what you are eating. It's hard to do that if you're reading or watching TV.

8. Try not to eat too much candy, cake, ice cream, and other sweet treats. Save them for special occasions.

9. Don't eat chocolate before you go to bed. The sugar and caffeine it contains get you wired and make it harder to go to sleep.

The Value of Exercise

Exercise is so important for every part of your body as well as your mind. It helps maintain your muscle mass, which means you'll have a healthy, active metabolism and will burn the calories you eat.

Good options include taking exercise classes at the local Y, biking, running, walking, participating in sports, skating. Use your Wii, which has exercise programs that include yoga, aerobics, and weight training—the programs can be customized to be just what you need.

Try to work some exercise into your daily routine. Walking to school instead of taking a bus or a ride, using the stairs instead of the elevator, will increase your level of fitness and don't involve making a special time for a workout. Weight-bearing exercise like walking or running is important to maintain healthy bones.

Why You Should Avoid Dieting

There are many reasons that dieting is not good for people, especially at your age, when your body is changing so quickly. What matters more than being thin is being healthy. A person can be full-figured and still be physically fit. But this requires healthy eating and enough exercise.

Dieting or taking diet pills that take away your appetite and make you jittery and nervous is not the way to lose weight. The weight never stays off because no one can stay on a diet for very long. Dieting can deprive your body of vitamins, minerals, and other nutrients that are essential to you, especially now. You can become addicted to diet pills and that can have a negative effect on your body and your mind.

Because dieting affects your metabolism (the process by which our bodies burn up the calories we eat), when you fall off a diet, the weight you lost comes right back on, faster than when you lost it. As I have said, the true way to weight loss and health is a combination of eating a healthy diet (different from dieting) and playing sports or doing some sort of regular physical exercise. Even if obesity runs in your family, it is possible for you to overcome it through healthy eating and exercise.

Overcoming Obesity or Being Overweight

Being overweight means there is too much fat in your body. Being overweight can lead to obesity, which means that the excess fat may lead to health problems such as diabetes, asthma, and trouble with bones and joints, as well as high blood pressure and heart disease. Obesity is a real strain on the body.

Overcoming obesity is hard to do on your own, especially since some of the main causes of obesity have to do with whether your parents are obese, what kinds of foods you are given at home and at school, and whether you are encouraged by your parents, guardians, or grandparents to be physically active.

But since obesity is a very real health hazard, let's look at some of the things you can do about it:

- Stop drinking soda at home or at school. These sugary soft drinks are a big contributor to childhood obesity.
- Stop eating fatty snacks and fast foods and eat more of the healthier foods I have listed above.

- Do all you can to be more physically active:
  - o Walk instead of ride.
  - o Climb stairs instead of taking the elevator or escalator.
  - o Schedule time to take a fifteen-minute walk three to five times a week.
  - o Try swimming, dancing, biking.
  - o Don't spend all your time playing computer or video games or watching television.

If you are overweight, it isn't easy to get started with physical activity, but if you can keep at it, it gets easier and you will keep feeling better and better. Better, in fact, than you ever imagined you could.

Resources

You might ask a doctor or school nurse if he or she knows of a local program that helps adolescents who suffer from obesity. There are a number of programs available to overweight and obese teens. One example is the Optimum Weight for Life program at the Children's Hospital in Boston. Most major cities will have a similar obesity prevention and treatment program. Ask your medical provider for a referral if you are ready to start such a program.

20.

Eating Disorders

Somewhere between five and ten million girls in the United States—about one in five—and possibly as many as one million boys have eating disorders.

What Is an Eating Disorder?

An eating disorder, like alcoholism, is a disease, not a sign of personal weakness. In fact, many—maybe even a majority—of girls and women who suffer from eating disorders are disciplined high achievers who get good grades and are popular. Perhaps it's the "pleasers"—those most concerned with pleasing others—who are most vulnerable to this addiction. About half of people with eating disorders also suffer from depression.

The pressure to rigidly conform and having no way to express yourself can trigger an eating disorder. So can feeling out of control in your life and needing to find something you can control—your eating. Other stress- and anxiety-causing events that can be triggers might include the death of a parent or a beloved pet, divorce in the family, the end of a relationship, or any kind of sexual abuse or rape—now or earlier in childhood.

Most people who suffer with eating disorders, however, have no trigger at all. Eating disorders tend to run in families, and you may be at risk simply because of your family history, rather than because of some stress or trigger in your life.

The Dangers of Eating Disorders

Eating disorders can cause later serious problems with the kidneys, intestines, throat, and glands; it can affect your metabolism and menstrual cycle, and cause dental problems.

Like any other addiction, an eating disorder makes it impossible to have a true, authentic relationship with anyone, including yourself. A teenager with an eating disorder may have a girlfriend or boyfriend, but it's not likely to be an authentic, satisfying relationship, one in which he or she is fully present, not thinking about something else, like food. The all-consuming, antisocial, addictive nature of eating disorders leads to depression, loss of self-esteem, hostility, fatigue, being obsessive, or being secretive. These are things that only serve to drive a wedge between people, even loved ones.

Types of Eating Disorders

Anorexia

Anorexia nervosa is an eating disorder in which sufferers severely restrict how much they eat in an effort to lose weight. It is very difficult to treat and has the highest fatality rate of all the psychiatric illnesses. Boys as well as girls suffer from anorexia.

Girls and boys who suffer from anorexia may also be trying to postpone becoming fully mature women and men. For example, girls can become so thin that they are sexless, because they stop having periods.

Over time, an anorexic's bones may stick out and their skin and hair become dull, dry, and brittle. They have distended bellies, they stop menstruating, grow weak, depressed, and negative. Their entire lives revolve around avoiding food. The disease is very serious and can result in hospitalization or even death.

Bulimia

Bulimia involves binging, which is eating a large amount of food at one time and then purging, or cleaning out the food, by throwing up or using laxatives to expel food before it is fully digested.

There are horrendous downsides to this disease and absolutely no upside. Bulimics think they will lose weight, but it's an illusion. Inevitably, bulimia damages your metabolism and bodily functions so seriously that anything you eat will cause you to gain weight. Teeth are sometimes so damaged from the stomach acid when throwing up that they need to be removed and replaced.

Compulsive Eating

Some girls and boys binge, like bulimics, but do not purge. This is called *compulsive eating*. They do this to numb themselves against pain and anxiety. Victims of sexual abuse sometimes do this to arm themselves against unwanted approaches. They hide within their fat.

Mary Pipher describes compulsive eating in her book about teenage girls, *Reviving Ophelia:* "Compulsive overeaters are often young women [or men] with a history of dieting. They diet and feel miserable, then they eat and feel better, but meanwhile their dieting makes their metabolism grow more and more sluggish. Over time weight loss becomes associated with control, and weight gain with out-of-control behavior. They become more obsessed with calories and weight. Soon, it is not just their eating but their lives that are out of control." (Mary Pipher, *Reviving Ophelia: Saving the Selves of Adolescent Girls.* New York: Riverhead, p. 179.)

If You or a Friend Has an Eating Disorder

Seek help from someone trained specifically in dealing with eating disorders. Just addressing eating habits and nutrition won't cut it. You don't binge and purge (or just binge) because you crave food. Though you may not realize it just yet, it is emotional and spiritual things you crave, not food. I believe—and this is very important to think about—that it is your lost self that you crave. It is no coincidence that eating disorders usually begin at the same time that girls and boys begin to try to become popular and fit in and lose touch with who they really are.

To get over an eating disorder, it is important for you to get your real self back (stop faking), and this may not be easy without the help of a professional person trained in dealing with eating disorders. Many youths benefit from meeting with a therapist in groups of other young people. Talking about it with others who also suffer with food addictions helps you to understand the triggers, the feelings, that cause it. Sometimes, the twelve-step program that originated with Alcoholics Anonymous is helpful. But whether it is that program or another one, you need help to develop the tools, the skills, to face your feelings, recover from the psychic pain that has led to your addiction, and get yourself back. There is a list of resources to turn to at the end of this chapter.

You will tend to resist getting help because your image of yourself is so distorted that you don't see the sickly creature you have become. This denial of reality is called "body dysmorphic disorder." Eating feels too unsafe, too out of control. But you need to realize that anorexia is not your friend but your enemy . . . perhaps your mortal enemy.

If you think you have anorexia or bulimia, ask your parents or your school counselor to arrange for you to see your doctor. The most important thing is to be sure you are safe and do not need to be in the hospital. The doctor will check your heart and do some blood and urine tests to make sure your bodily systems are functioning okay. You may need to be in a hospital to get your body to a safe place before you start a program to address your eating disorder. Most teenagers with eating disorders will start treatment in a "day program" where you will spend a good part of the day getting help. If that's not enough, you may be admitted to an overnight eating disorders program. An example of an inpatient eating disorders program is the Klarman Center for Eating Disorders at McClean Hospital near Boston. Look at their website to learn about how these programs work: www .mclean.harvard.edu/patient/child/edc.php

It's so important to ask for help in order to stop feeling

weak and worthless! What getting help shows, instead, is that you are a smart person who wants to be good to him- or herself. Recovery doesn't happen overnight. But it does happen!

As with bulimia and anorexia, compulsive overeating can be helped by joining a support group such as Overeaters Anonymous. A self-help tool for Overeaters Anonymous and other twelve-step programs is: HALT—Don't get too Hungry, Angry, Lonely, or Tired.

Resources

- Overeaters Anonymous: On the website you are likely to find a location near you. Meeting information line: 1–505–891–2664
  www.oa.org

- The Renfrew Center 1–800–RENFREW: the country's first residential eating-disorder treatment facility that specializes solely in the treatment of anorexia, bulimia, and binge-eating disorder
  www.renfrewcenter.com

- The Walker Wellness Clinic: 1–877–899–7254
  www.walkerwellness.com

- Anorexia Nervosa and Related Eating Disorders (ANRED)
  www.anred.com

- National Eating Disorders Association (NEDA)
  www.nationaleatingdisorders.org
  Eating disorders information and referrals line:
  1–800–931–2237

- Academy of Eating Disorders
  aedweb.org

- Eating Disorders Online
  www.eatingdisordersonline.com

- National Association for Males with Eating
  Disorders
  www.NAMEDinc.org

- National Association of Anorexia Nervosa and
  Associated Disorders
  anad.org

- The Gail R. Schoenbach F.R.E.E.D. Foundation
  freedfoundation.org

- Eating Disorder Referral and Information Center
  www.edreferral.com

- Center for Young Women's Health: "Health information for teen girls around the world"
  www.youngwomenshealth.org/eating_disorders.html

- About-Face!: a nonprofit organization focusing on
  positive body image and body acceptance
  www.about-face.org

Putting It All Together

I hope you have found this book useful. Remember that you can dip into it from time to time to remind yourself of how to handle situations that may come up, things that may not have seemed important to you the first time around.

Here are the key ideas I hope you remember:

1. Your body is still developing and you have a right to understand how it is changing.
2. Your body is sacred. It is not to be feared, nor should you feel shame or guilt regarding your body, no matter what.
3. Most girls and boys in high school are not having sex. Abstaining from sexual intercourse at your age is the best way to reduce your risk of pregnancy and infection.
4. If you start having sex, be sure you are able to discuss contraception with your partner and use it correctly *every single time.*

5. Do not start having sex just because your friends say they are sexually active.

6. Being with someone you trust and can communicate with, besides someone who turns you on, helps ensure your experience will be pleasurable.

7. You can say "no" to any form of sex—kissing, touching, anything—*anytime you feel like it, for any reason.*

8. If you have been sexually abused, assaulted, or harassed, it was not your fault. You need to talk to a trusted adult and report what has happened to you.

9. You and your partner are both responsible for talking about feelings and asking about feelings.

10. Boys and girls are both responsible for seeking each other's permission before any sexual touching advances.

11. Find a trustworthy adult to talk to if you have questions about your reproductive health or mental health. Avoid getting all your advice from your young friends or on the Internet.

12. This is the time in your life when you should begin to figure out who you are as a person, who you want to be, what values you claim for yourself.

I hope this book has helped answer your questions about your changing body, relationships, being a sexual person, and being responsible.

With this book, I send love and encouragement.

Acknowledgments

Many people assisted me with this book. I want to thank, first and foremost, my editor, Kate Medina, associate publisher at Random House.

Lindsey Schwoeri was also my editor and her help was generous and invaluable.

Beverly Horowitz, publisher of Random House Children's Books, provided help and advice at every step along the way.

My thanks also to Benjamin Dreyer, Leigh Marchant, Sally Marvin, Tom Perry, Anna Pitoniak, Robbin Schiff, and Theresa Zoro at Random House. And to Gina Centrello, president and publisher of Random House.

My thanks to Julia Rothman, who created the illustrations throughout the book, and to Dr. Eileen Costello for her reading of the book.

Special thanks to Dr. Lisa Bennett for being my consulting psychologist and for jump-starting this undertaking.

To be sure I was on the right track and got course correction when needed, I gave the manuscript to a number of teenagers along the way who were honest and forthcoming in their feedback: Aviv Chaim Lis, Zach Kimmel, Amy Kimmel, Charlie Levy, Eli Levy, Kassie Spain, Kathryn Foley, Nat Wolfe, the Keenan family, and Luke Browning. I am grateful for their time and feedback. Much gratitude as well to Alyssa Tartaglione, who helped with research.

Two amazing men were generous with their help when it came to writing about boys:

Paul Kivel, educator, activist, and writer on issues that include teen dating, family violence, and raising boys to manhood. His books include *Men's Work: How to Stop the Violence That Tears Our Lives Apart* and *Boys Will Be Men*.

And Dr. Michael Kimmel, Distinguished Professor of Sociology at Stony Brook University in New York and a leader in the field of men's studies whose books include *Guyland: The Perilous World Where Boys Become Men*.

My friend the Reverend Debra W. Haffner was beyond generous whenever I asked for advice. She is cofounder and president of the Religious Institute, a sexologist, and an ordained Unitarian minister who has written numerous wonderful books on parenting, including *From Diapers to Dating, Beyond the Big Talk,* and *What Every 21st-Century Parent Needs to Know*.

With her important book *Dilemmas of Desire: Teenage Girls Talk About Sexuality,* Deborah L. Tolman helped me understand why girls who are made to fear their sexual desire are put at risk. Deborah is professor of social welfare and psychology at the Silberman School of Social Work at Hunter College. She cofounded SPARK, an intergenerational, girl-fueled movement-building organization dedicated to challenging the sexualization of girls in the media and beyond.

My thanks to Kim Nolte, vice president of programs and training for the Georgia Campaign for Adolescent Power & Potential. Under Kim's guidance, scores of teens throughout Georgia read my manuscript and gave their on-the-ground and often startling feedback.

My friend the Reverend Bill Stayton was professor in the Satcher Health Leadership Institute at the Morehouse School of Medicine, professor emeritus and former director of sexuality studies at Widener University, and serves as an adjunct professor at the University of Minnesota Medical School. Bill is an ordained American Baptist clergyman. He and his wife, Kathy, read this book along the way and provided essential feedback and advice.

Yolanda Turner, assistant professor of psychology at Eastern University in Pennsylvania, helped me in addressing issues of gender identity, as did my dear friend Calpernia Addams, author, actress, and a spokesperson and activist for transgender rights and issues.

Dr. Melissa Kottke, assistant professor of gynecology and obstetrics, is the medical director at the Jane Fonda Center for Adolescent Reproductive Health at the Emory University School of Medicine in Atlanta. She held roundtable discussions on this book and gave deeply of her help and expertise.

And, finally, I must thank Donna Rohling. While she was on the board of the Georgia Campaign for Adolescent Pregnancy Prevention (since renamed the Georgia Campaign for Adolescent Power & Potential) and raising a young son, she suggested I write this book. And I did.

Resource Guide

Resources for Girls' Empowerment

Rookie

www.rookiemag.com

An online magazine by teens, for teens that covers a wide range of topics, from music, movies, and tech to love and sex and more from a progressive, feminist perspective.

V-Girls

www.v-girls.org

A global network of girl activists and advocates inspired by Eve Ensler's bestselling book *I Am an Emotional Creature: The Secret Life of Girls.*

The Dressing Room Project

www.thedressingroomproject.org/index.html

A girl-powered rebellion to free girls and women from media-imposed standards of beauty.

The Spark Movement
www.sparkmovement.org

A girl-fueled activist movement that collaborates with hundreds of girls ages 13–22 and more than 60 national organizations to end the sexualization of women and girls in media.

New Moon
www.newmoon.com/magazine

A magazine written by and for girls ages 8–14, with intelligent and fun articles about issues important to girls.

Resources for Boys' Empowerment

Boys to Men International
www.boystomen.org

An organization that offers mentoring for boys ages 12–17.

Health Initiatives for Youth
www.hify.org

Check out the guide *The Dangerous Book for Boys* by Conn Iggulden and Hal Iggulden (New York: William Morrow, 2012).

100 Things Guys Need to Know by Bill Zimmerman (Minneapolis, Minn.: Free Spirit Publishing, 2005).

Sexuality, STI and Pregnancy Prevention, and More

Go Ask Alice!

www.goaskalice.columbia.edu

An online resource for teens to ask questions and get honest answers about sex, relationships, and health in general, run by Columbia University. You can write in your own question, or read others' questions.

Planned Parenthood

www.plannedparenthood.org
1–800–230–PLAN (1–800–230–7526)

Offers reproductive health care, sex education, and information. Clinics are located all over the United States. Services are low-cost and sometimes free.

Advocates for Youth

www.advocatesforyouth.org

An organization dedicated to sexuality education, HIV and sexually transmitted disease prevention, teenage pregnancy prevention, youth access to condoms and contraception, and equality for LGBTQ youth.

Sex in the States

www.sexetc.org/action-center/sex-in-the-states

Provides information about young people's rights to sex education, birth control, access to abortion, and more, arranged by

state. Run by *Sex, etc.,* a magazine for teens, by teens that offers honest and accurate sexual health information.

National Council for Adoption
   www.adoptioncouncil.org
   1–202–328–1200

National Adoption Information Clearinghouse
   www.adoption.org
   1–703–352–3488 or 1–888–251–0075

Eva B. Donaldson Adoption Institute
   www.adoptioninstitute.org/research/domesticadoption.php

Resources for Lesbian, Gay, Bisexual, Transgender or Questioning (LGBTQ) Youth

The Hetrick-Martin Institute
   www.hmi.org
   1–212–674–2400

An organization devoted to serving the needs of LGBTQ
youth.

The Gay, Lesbian, Straight Education Network (GLSEN)
   www.glsen.org

An organization that works to end discrimination, harassment, and bullying based on sexual orientation, gender identity, and gender expression in K-12 schools.

Advocates for Youth

www.advocatesforyouth.org

An organization dedicated to sexuality education, HIV and sexually transmitted disease prevention, teenage pregnancy prevention, youth access to condoms and contraception, and equality for LGBTQ youth.

The Trevor Project

www.thetrevorproject.org
1–866–4–U–TREVOR (1–866–488–7386)

An organization determined to end suicide among LBGTQ youth by providing resources and a nationwide, 24-hour hotline. If you are considering suicide or need help, call now.

It Gets Better

www.itgetsbetter.org/video

Thousands of videos submitted by people across the country to inspire and encourage LGBT youth who are struggling.

Parents, Families & Friends of Lesbians and Gays (PFLAG)

www.pflag.org

National Youth Advocacy Coalition

www.nyacyouth.org

The Point Foundation

www.pointfoundation.org

Offers mentorship, leadership development, and community service training to lesbian, gay, bisexual, transgender and queer (LGBTQ) students.

Lambda Legal
   www.lambdalegal.org

Offers LGBTQ legal resources.

The Mpowerment Project
   www.mpowerment.org

An HIV prevention program for young gay and bisexual men.

TransYouth Family Allies (TYFA)
   www.imatyfa.org

Indiana Youth Group
   www.indianayouthgroup.org
   1–800–347–TEEN (8336)

Recognizing and Ending Unhealthy Relationships

Love Is Respect.org
   www.loveisrespect.org

An organization dedicated to engaging, educating, and empowering youth and young adults to prevent and end abusive relationships. In addition to the helpful information on its website, Love Is Respect has a National Dating Abuse Helpline that teens can access 24/7 by text, phone, or online chat. Text "love is" to 77052, call 1–866–331–9474, or visit www.loveis respect.org/about-national-dating-abuse-helpline.

Start Strong: Building Healthy Teen Relationships
www.startstrongteens.org
1–415–678–5500

Through this website and phone line, your parents or teachers can access a workshop called "Moving from a Relationship Bystander to a Relationship Upstander."

Break the Cycle: Empowering Youth to End Domestic Violence
www.breakthecycle.org

Love Is Not Abuse
www.loveisnotabuse.com

Ending Sexual Abuse

National Child Abuse Hotline
1–800–4–A–CHILD (1–800–422–4453)

National Sexual Assault Hotline
1–800–656–HOPE (1–800–656–4673)

National Coalition Against Sexual Assault
1–717–728–9764

Rape, Abuse, and Incest National Network (RAINN)
www.rainn.org
1–800–656–HOPE (1–800–656–4673)

Safe Horizon

www.safehorizon.org

1–212–227–3000 (New York Center)

1–203–785–2540 (Yale Center)

Have a parent get in touch with Safe Horizons, a victims' assistance group with centers in New York City and at Yale University in New Haven, Connecticut. Safe Horizons has developed a proven therapy program for victims and their family members.

Mental Health and Counseling Services

Teen Mental Health

www.teenmentalhealth.org/for-families-and-teens

Medline Plus

www.nlm.nih.gov/medlineplus/teenmentalhealth.html

A service of the National Institutes of Health.

Bullying

StopBullying.gov

www.stopbullying.gov

The official U.S. Government website providing information and resources on how to prevent and stop bullying. Managed by the U.S. Department of Health & Human Services in partnership with the Department of Education and Department of Justice. A great resource for parents.

Teenangels.org
www.teenangels.org

An award-winning teen cybersafety group.

A Thin Line
www.athinline.org

An MTV campaign that was developed to empower individuals to identify, respond to, and stop the spread of digital abuse in their life and among their peers.

Striving to Reduce Youth Violence Everywhere (STRYVE)
www.vetoviolence.cdc.gov/stryve

A national initiative led by the Centers for Disease Control and Prevention (CDC) to prevent youth violence before it starts among young people ages 10–24.

National Bullying Prevention Center: Pacer Center's Teens Against Bullying
www.pacer.org/bullying

Facebook Safety Centre for Teens
www.facebook.com/safety/groups/teens

Helpful information about how to use Facebook safely.

Eating Disorders

The Renfrew Center
www.renfrewcenter.com
1–800–RENFREW

The country's first residential eating disorder treatment facility that specializes solely in the treatment of anorexia, bulimia, and binge-eating disorder.

National Eating Disorders Association (NEDA)
www.nationaleatingdisorders.org
1–800–931–2237

Overeaters Anonymous
www.oa.org
505–891–2664

A support group for compulsive overeaters. Find a meeting location near you on their website or by phone.

The Walker Wellness Center
www.walkerwellness.com
1–877–899–7254

Anorexia Nervosa and Related Eating Disorders, Inc. (ANRED)
www.anred.com

Eating Disorder Referral and Information Center
www.edreferral.com

Center for Young Women's Health
www.youngwomenshealth.org/eating_disorders.html

Health information for teen girls.

Index

About the Author

JANE FONDA, the Oscar- and Emmy-winning actor, is the founder of the Georgia Campaign for Adolescent Power & Potential and the Jane Fonda Center for Adolescent Reproductive Health at the Emory University School of Medicine. Though she is also a highly successful producer and #1 *New York Times* bestselling author, Fonda's passion lies in advocating for young people's health. She also sits on the boards of the Women and Foreign Policy at the Council on Foreign Relations, the Women's Media Center (which she co-founded in 2004), and V-Day. A former UN Goodwill Ambassador, she is a frequent speaker on youth development, child sexual abuse, eating disorders, adolescent reproductive health, and other topics. Jane Fonda lives in Los Angeles.

About the Type

This book was set in Garamond, a typeface originally designed by the Parisian type cutter Claude Garamond (c. 1500–61). This version of Garamond was modeled on a 1592 specimen sheet from the Egenolff-Berner foundry, which was produced from types assumed to have been brought to Frankfurt by the punch cutter Jacques Sabon (c. 1520–80).

Claude Garamond's distinguished romans and italics first appeared in *Opera Ciceronis* in 1543–44. The Garamond types are clear, open, and elegant.